CHRISTMAS SONGS for Banjo

Arranged by Jim Schustedt

ISBN-13: 978-1-4234-1397-4
ISBN-10: 1-4234-1397-0

HAL•LEONARD®
CORPORATION
7777 W. BLUEMOUND RD. P.O. BOX 13819 MILWAUKEE, WI 53213

In Australia Contact:
Hal Leonard Australia Pty. Ltd.
4 Lentara Court
Cheltenham, Victoria, 3192 Australia
Email: ausadmin@halleonard.com

Visit Hal Leonard Online at
www.halleonard.com

Angels We Have Heard on High

Traditional French Carol
Translated by James Chadwick

G tuning:
(5th-1st) G-D-G-B-D
Key of G

Intro
Moderately

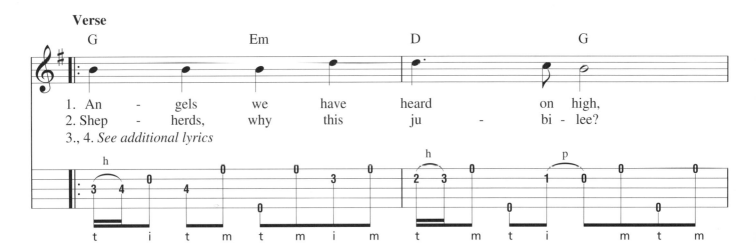

Verse

1. An - gels we have heard on high,
2. Shep - herds, why this ju - bi - lee?
3., 4. *See additional lyrics*

sweet - ly sing - ing o'er the plains.
Why your joy - ous strains pro - long?

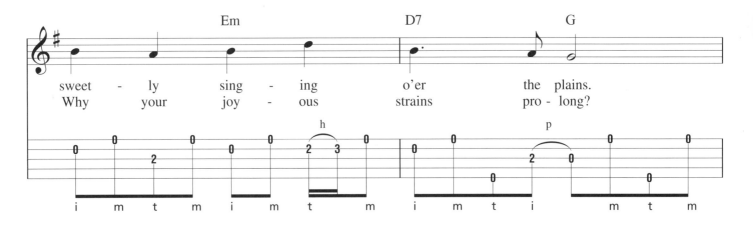

And the moun - tains in re - ply,
What the glad - some tid - ings be

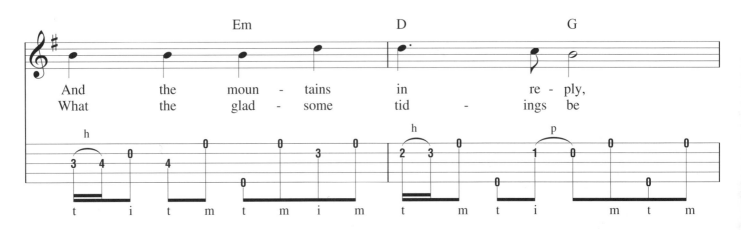

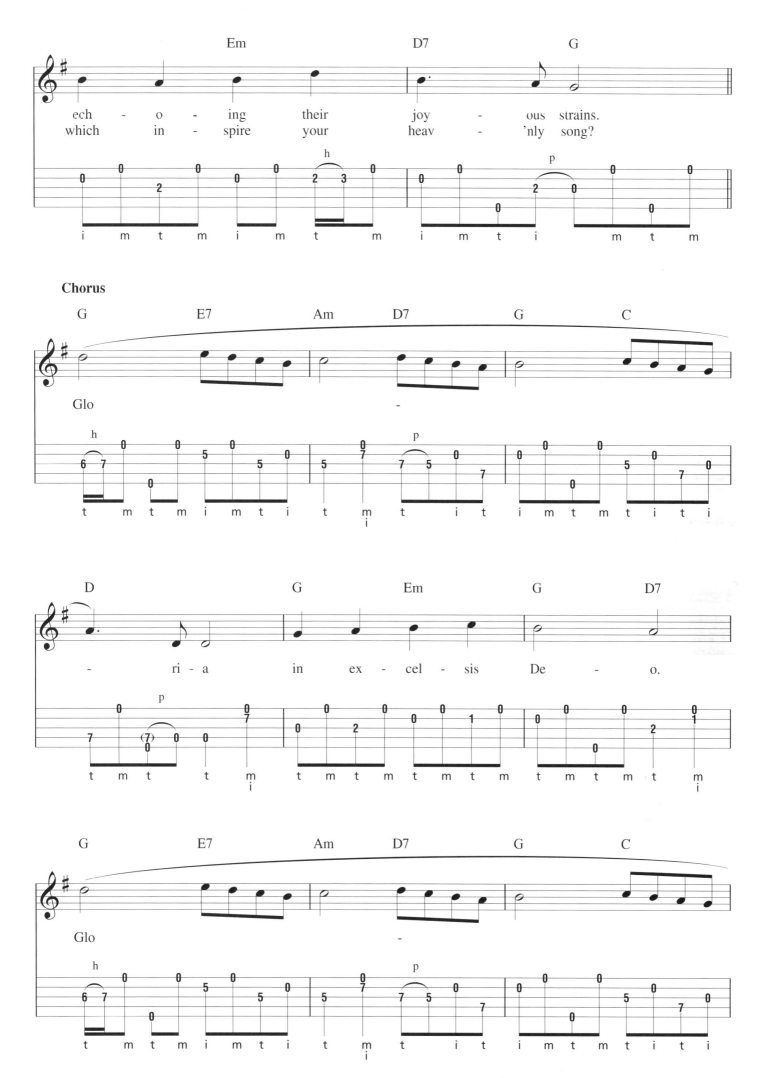

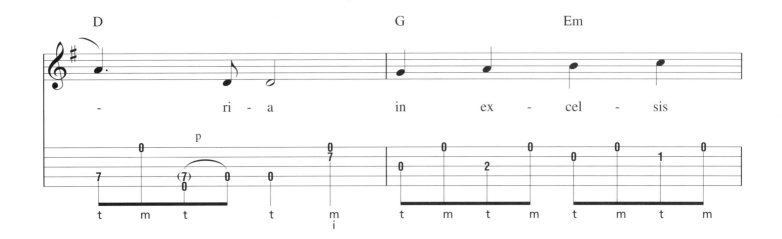

ri - a   in   ex - cel - sis

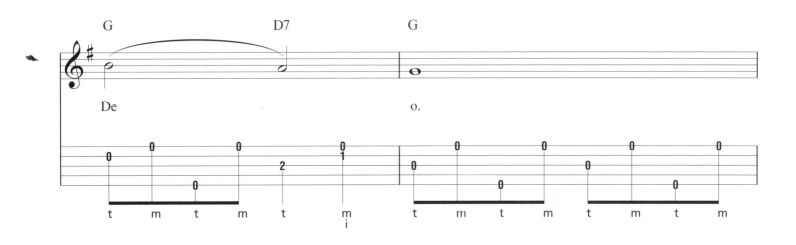

De   o.

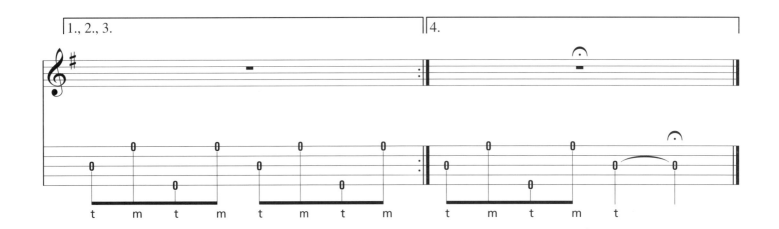

Additional Lyrics

3. Come to Bethlehem and see
   Him whose birth the angels sing;
   Come, adore on bended knee
   Christ the Lord, the newborn King.

4. See within a manger laid
   Jesus, Lord of heaven and earth!
   Mary, Joseph, lend your aid,
   With us sing our Savior's birth.

Carol of the Bells

Ukrainian Christmas Carol

G tuning:
(5th-1st) G-D-G-B-D

Key of Gm

Intro

Moderately fast

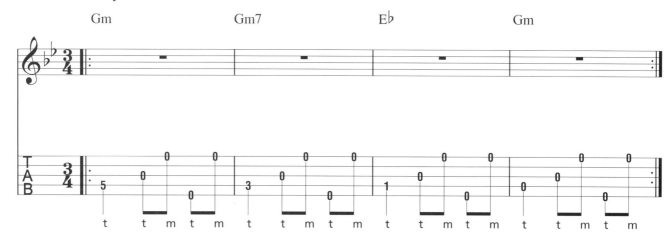

Verse

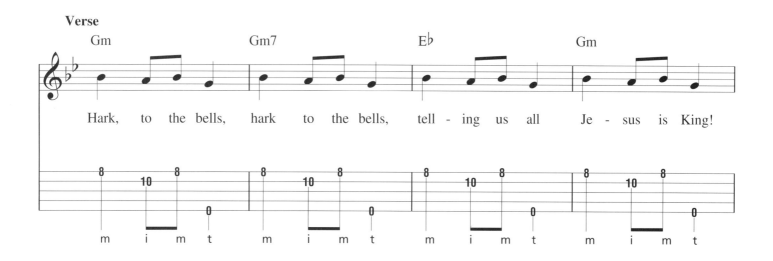

Hark, to the bells, hark to the bells, tell - ing us all Je - sus is King!

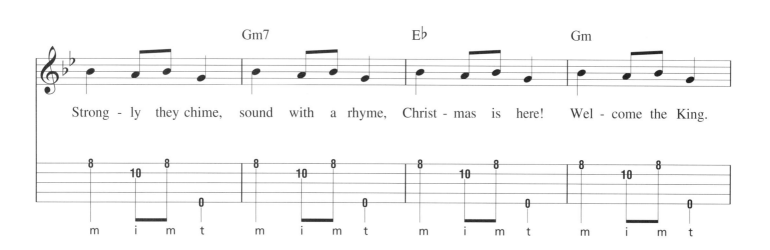

Strong - ly they chime, sound with a rhyme, Christ - mas is here! Wel - come the King.

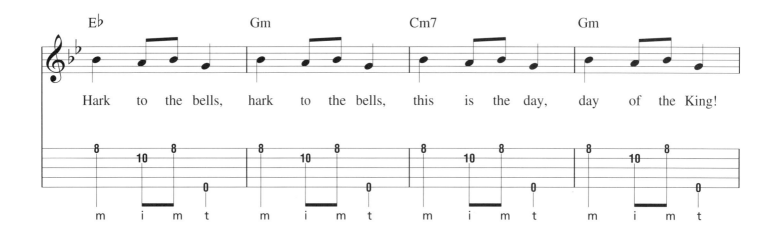

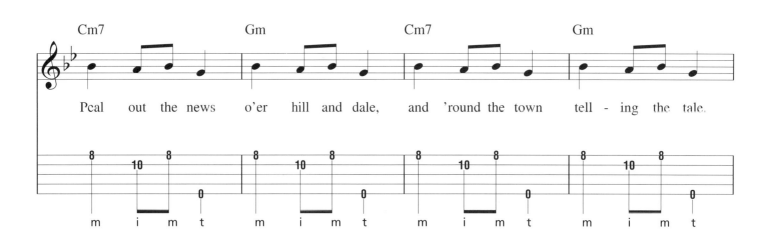

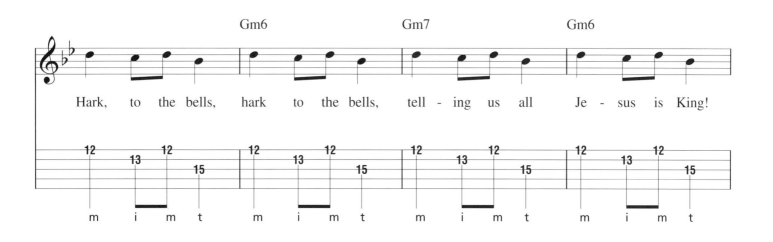

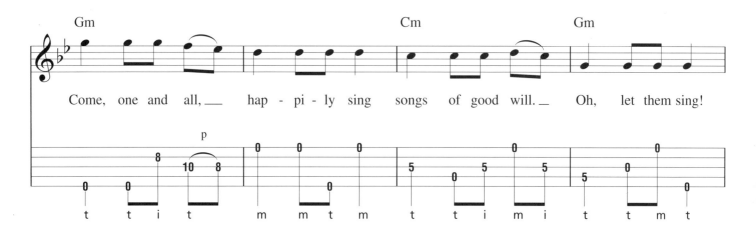

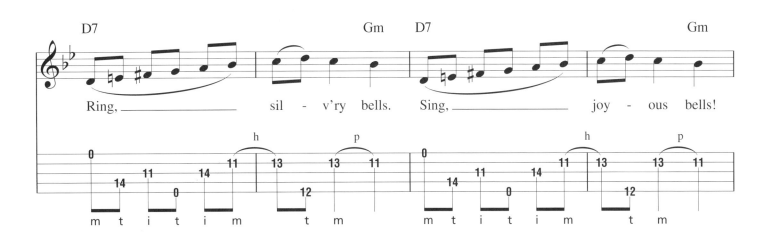

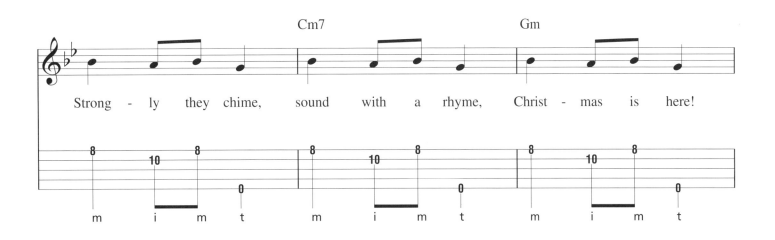

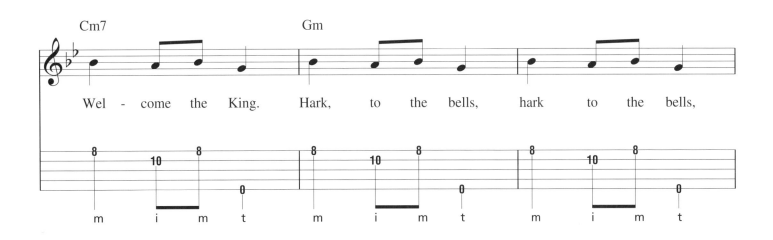

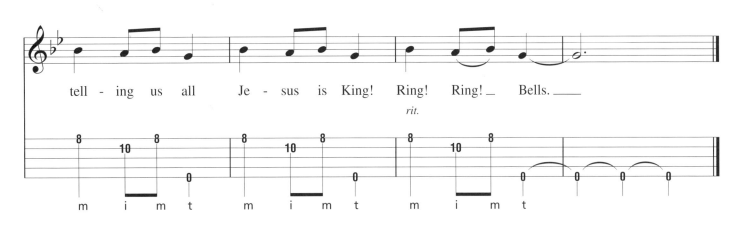

Away in a Manger

Traditional
Words by John T. McFarland (v.3)
Music by James R. Murray

G tuning:
(5th-1st) G-D-G-B-D

Key of G

Verse

Sweetly

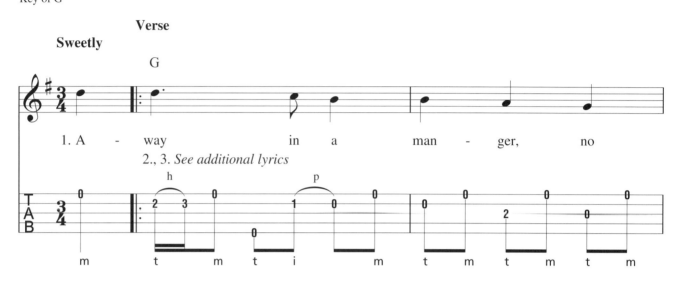

1. A - way in a man - ger, no
2., 3. *See additional lyrics*

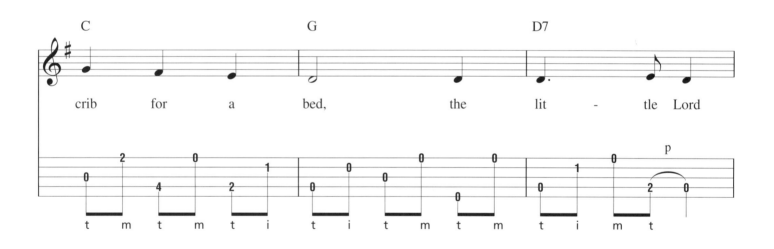

crib for a bed, the lit - tle Lord

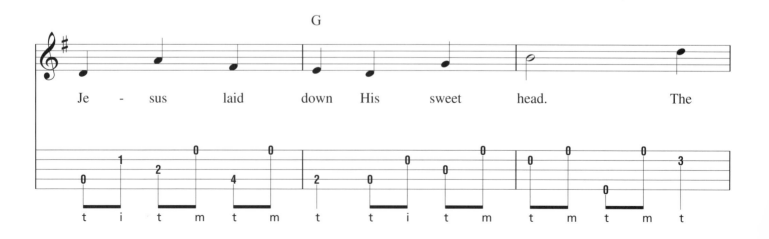

Je - sus laid down His sweet head. The

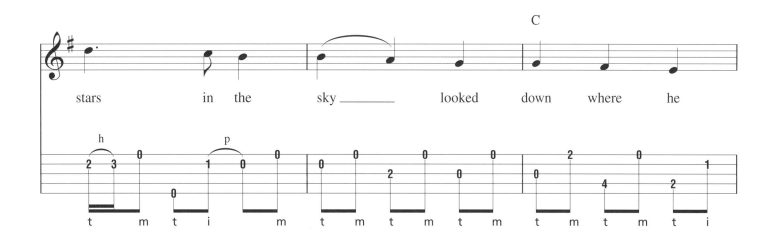

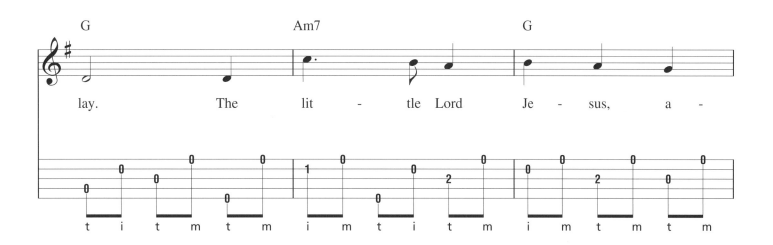

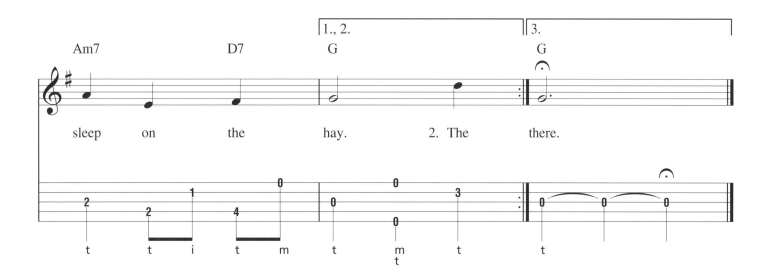

Additional Lyrics

2. The cattle are lowing, the baby awakes,
   But little Lord Jesus, no crying He makes.
   I love Thee, Lord Jesus, look down from the sky
   And stay by my cradle till morning is nigh.

3. Be near me, Lord Jesus, I ask Thee to stay
   Close by me forever and love me, I pray.
   Bless all the dear children in Thy tender care
   And fit us for heaven to live with Thee there.

Deck the Hall

Traditional Welsh Carol

G tuning:
(5th-1st) G-D-G-B-D

Key of G

Verse
Brightly

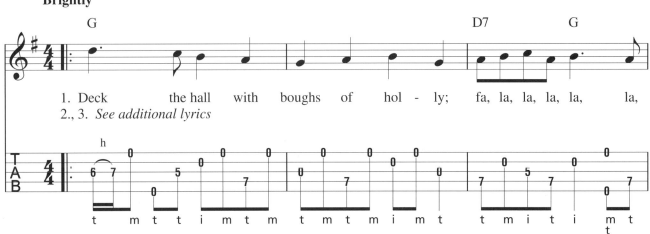

1. Deck the hall with boughs of hol - ly; fa, la, la, la, la, la,
2., 3. *See additional lyrics*

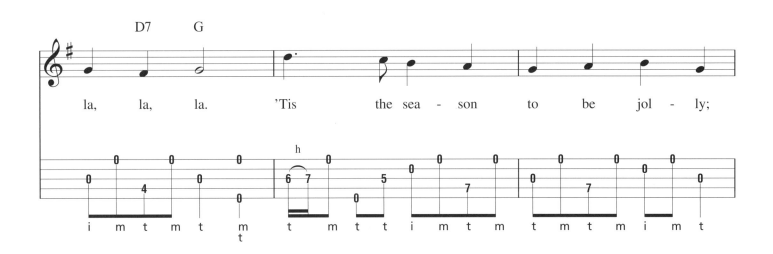

la, la, la. 'Tis the sea - son to be jol - ly;

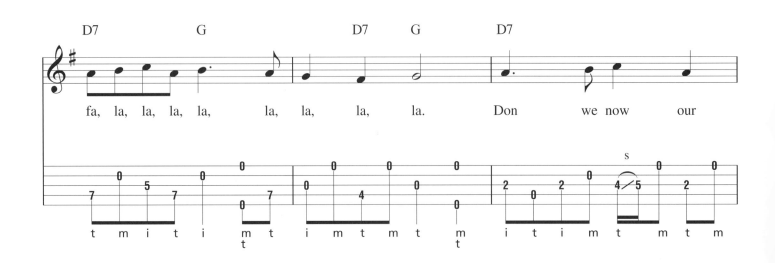

fa, la, la, la, la, la, la, la, la. Don we now our

Additional Lyrics

2. See the blazing yule before us;
Fa, la, la, la, la, la, la, la, la.
Strike the harp and join the chorus;
Fa, la, la, la, la, la, la, la, la.
Follow me in merry measure;
Fa, la, la, la, la, la, la, la, la.
While I tell of Yuletide treasure;
Fa, la, la, la, la, la, la, la, la.

3. Fast away the old year passes;
Fa, la, la, la, la, la, la, la, la.
Hail the new ye lads and lasses;
Fa, la, la, la, la, la, la, la, la.
Sing we joyous, all together;
Fa, la, la, la, la, la, la, la, la.
Heedless of the wind and weather;
Fa, la, la, la, la, la, la, la, la.

The First Noël

17th Century English Carol
Music from W. Sandy's *Christmas Carols*

G tuning:
(5th-1st) G-D-G-B-D

Key of G

Verse
Moderately slow

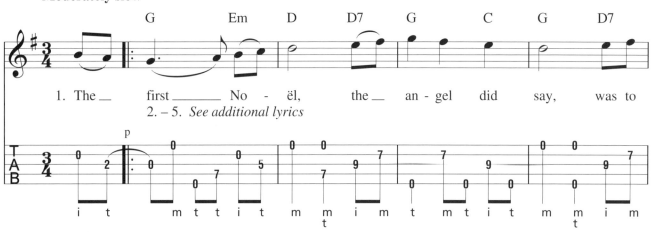

1. The __ first _____ No - ël, the __ an - gel did say, was to
2. – 5. *See additional lyrics*

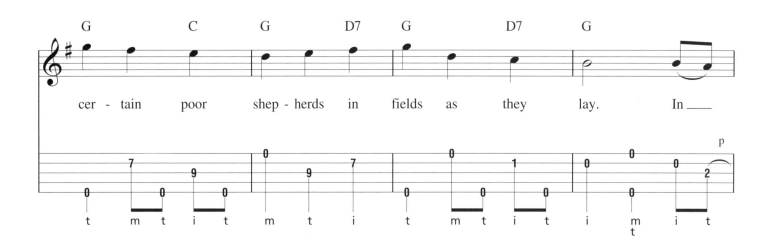

cer - tain poor shep - herds in fields as they lay. In ___

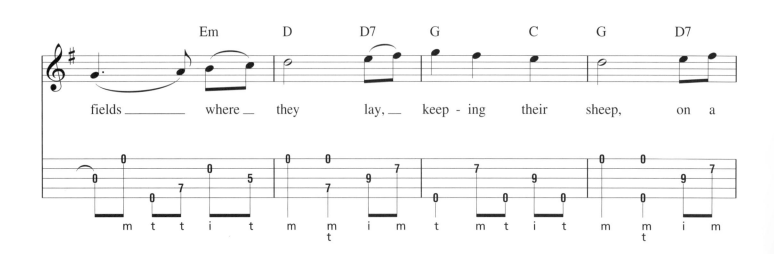

fields _____ where __ they lay, __ keep - ing their sheep, on a

Chorus

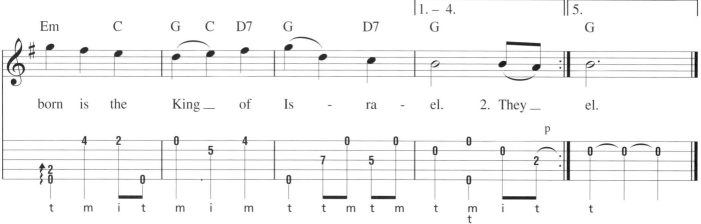

Additional Lyrics

2. They looked up and saw a star
   Shining in the east, beyond them far.
   And to the earth it gave great light
   And so it continued both day and night.

3. And by the light of that same star,
   Three wise men came from country far;
   To seek for a King was their intent,
   And to follow the star wherever it went.

4. This star drew nigh to the northwest,
   O'er Bethlehem it took its rest;
   And there it did both stop and stay,
   Right over the place where Jesus lay.

5. Then entered in those wise men three,
   Full reverently upon their knee;
   And offered there in His presence,
   Their gold, and myrrh, and frankincense.

Go, Tell It on the Mountain

African-American Spiritual
Verses by John W. Work, Jr.

G tuning:
(5th-1st) G-D-G-B-D
Key of G

Chorus
Moderately

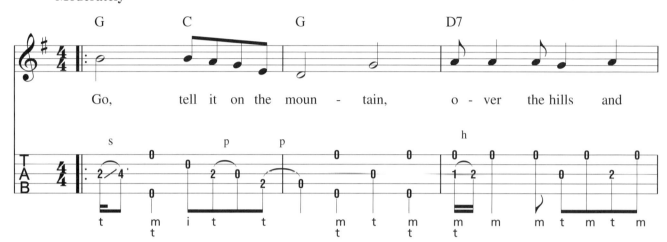

Go, tell it on the moun - tain, o - ver the hills and

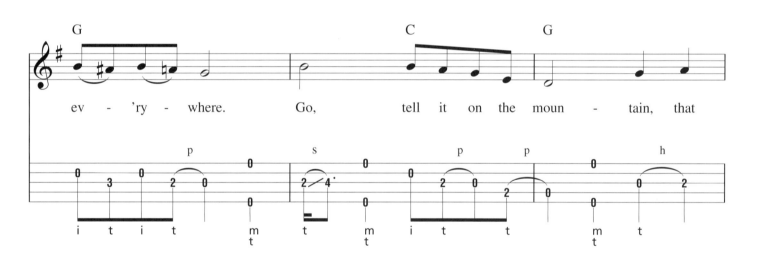

ev - 'ry - where. Go, tell it on the moun - tain, that

To Coda ⊕

Verse

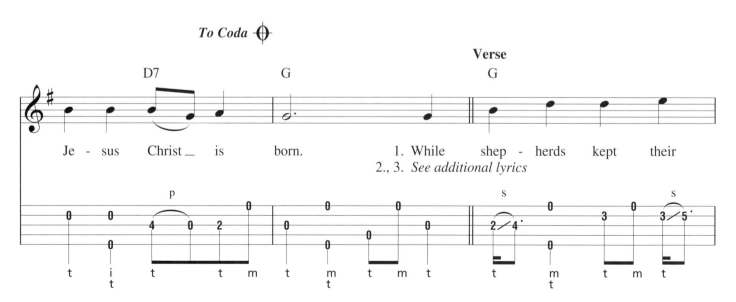

Je - sus Christ__ is born.
1. While shep - herds kept their
2., 3. *See additional lyrics*

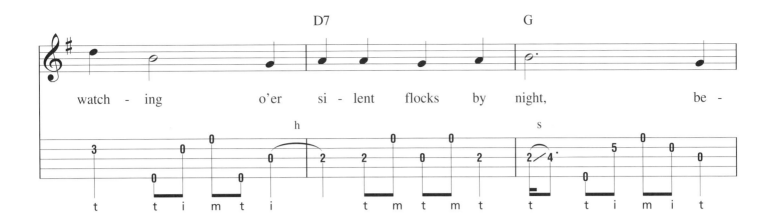

watch - ing   o'er   si - lent   flocks   by   night,   be -

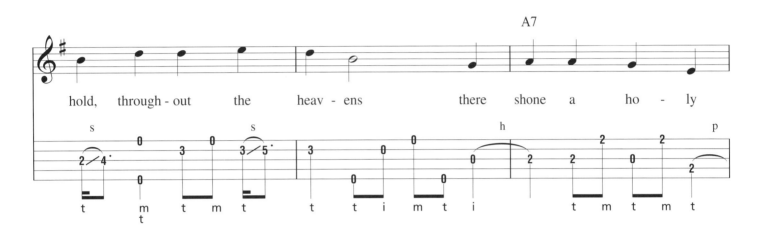

hold,   through - out   the   heav - ens   there   shone   a   ho - ly

1., 2. | 3.

D.C. al Coda

◆ Coda

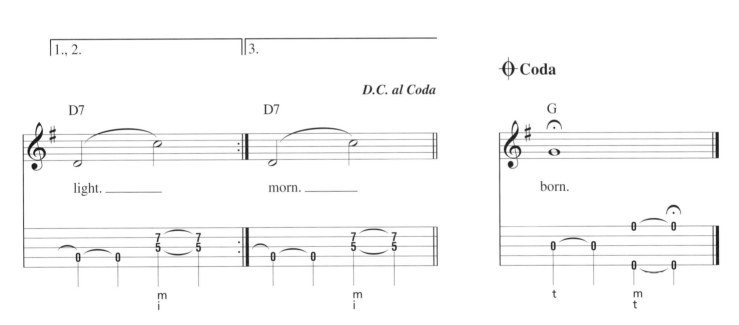

light. _____   morn. _____

born.

Additional Lyrics

2. The shepherds feared and trembled
   When, lo! above the earth
   Rang out the angel chorus
   That hailed our Savior's birth.

3. Down in a lowly manger
   Our humble Christ was born.
   And God sent us salvation
   That blessed Christmas morn.

God Rest Ye Merry, Gentlemen

19th Century English Carol

G minor tuning:
(5th-1st) G-D-G-B♭-D

Key of Gm

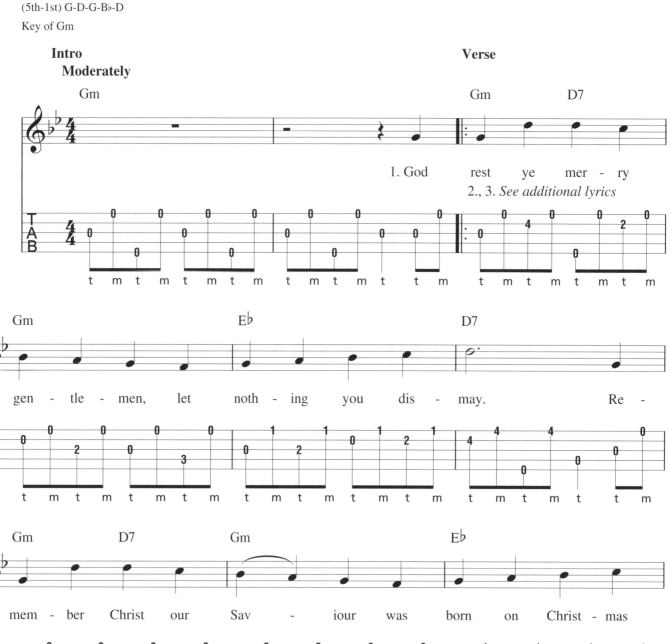

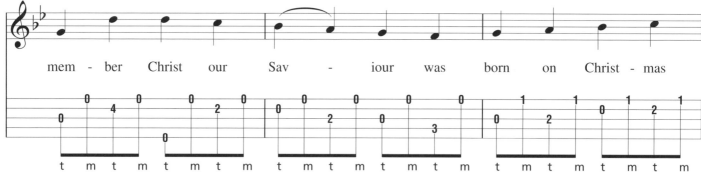

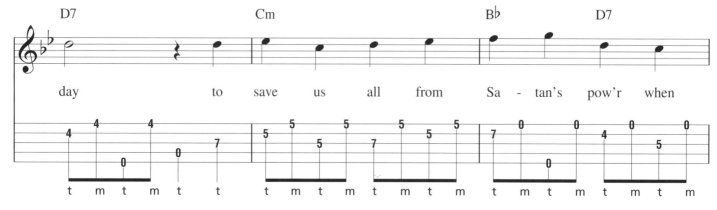

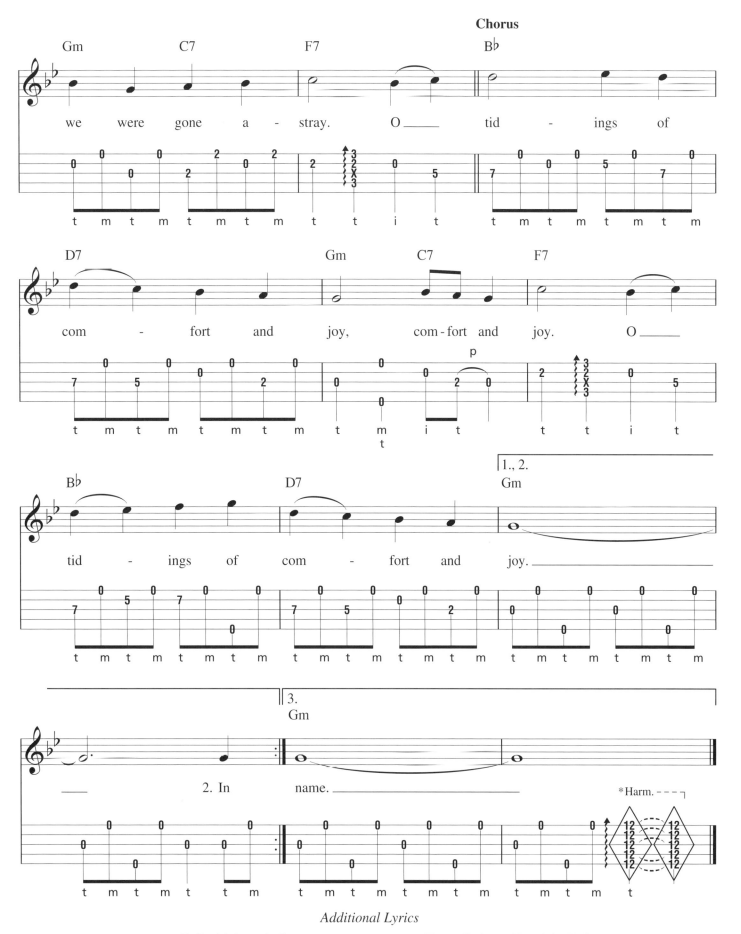

Additional Lyrics

In Bethlehem, in Jewry,
2. This blessed Babe was born,
And laid within a manger
Upon this blessed morn
That which His mother Mary
Did nothing take in scorn.

From God, our Heav'nly Father,
3. A blessed angel came,
And unto certain shepherds
Brought tidings of the same.
How that in Bethlehem was born
The Son of God by name.

*Harmonics are produced by picking the notes while the fret-hand lightly touches the strings directly over the fret indicated.

Good King Wenceslas

Words by John M. Neale
Music from Piae Cantiones

G tuning:
(5th-1st) G-D-G-B-D

Key of G

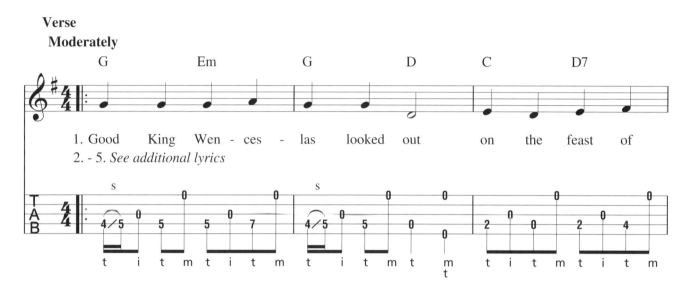

1. Good King Wen - ces - las looked out on the feast of
2. - 5. *See additional lyrics*

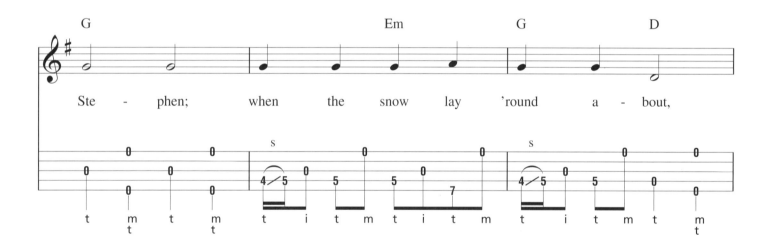

Ste - phen; when the snow lay 'round a - bout,

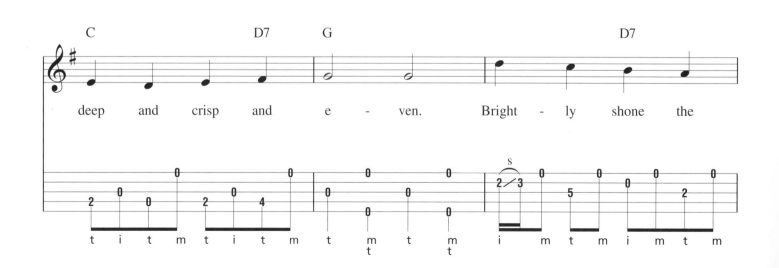

deep and crisp and e - ven. Bright - ly shone the

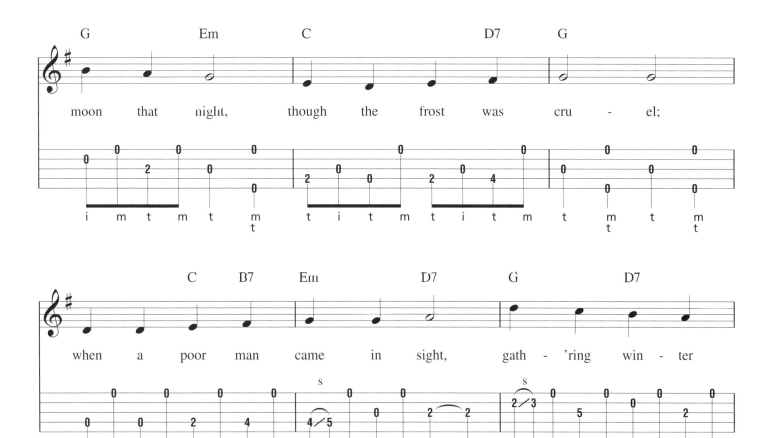

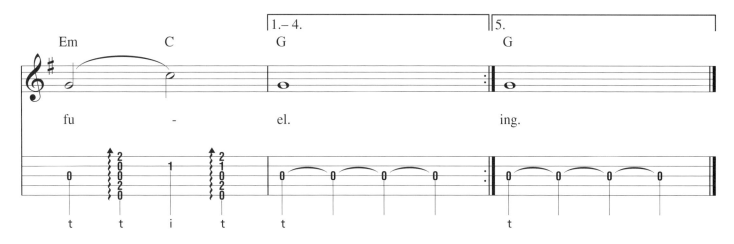

Additional Lyrics

2. "Hither page, and stand by me,
   If thou know'st it telling;
   Yonder peasent, who is he?
   Where and what his dwelling?"
   "Sire, he lives a good league hence,
   Underneath the mountain;
   Right against the forest fence,
   By Saint Agnes fountain."

3. "Bring me flesh, and bring me wine,
   Bring me pine-logs hither;
   Thou and I will see him dine,
   When we bear then thither."
   Page and monarch forth they went,
   Forth they went together;
   Through the rude winds wild lament,
   And the bitter weather.

4. "Sire, the night is darker now,
   And the wind blows stronger;
   Fails my heart, I know not how,
   I can go not longer."
   "Mark my footsteps, my good page,
   Tread thou in them boldly;
   Thou shalt find the winter's rage
   Freeze thy blood less coldly."

5. In his master's steps he trod,
   Where the snow lay dinted;
   Heat was in the very sod
   Which the saint has printed.
   Therefore, Christmas men, be sure,
   Wealth or rank possessing;
   Ye who now will bless the poor,
   Shall yourselves find blessing.

Hark! The Herald Angels Sing

Words by Charles Wesley
Altered by George Whitefield
Music by Felix Mendelssohn-Bartholdy

G tuning:
(5th-1st) G-D-G-B-D
Key of G

Verse
Moderately

1. Hark! The her - ald an - gels sing, ___ "Glo - ry to the
2., 3. *See additional lyrics*

new - born King! Peace on earth, and mer - cy mild, ___

God and sin - ners re - con - ciled." Joy - ful all ye

na - tions rise. ___ Join the tri - umph of the skies. ___

Additional Lyrics

2. Christ, by highest heav' adored, Christ, the everlasting Lord;
   Late in time behold Him come, offspring of the virgin's womb.
   Veil'd in flesh the Godhead see. Hail th'Incarnate Deity.
   Pleased as man with man to dwell, Jesus our Emmanuel!
   Hark! The herald angels sing, "Glory to the newborn King!"

3. Hail, the heav'n born Prince of Peace! Hail, the Son of Righteousness!
   Light and life to all He brings, ris'n with healing in His wings.
   Mild He lays His glory by. Born that man no more may die.
   Born to raise the sons of earth, born to give them second birth.
   Hark! The herald angels sing, "Glory to the newborn King!"

I Saw Three Ships

Traditional English Carol

G tuning:
(5th-1st) G-D-G-B-D

Key of G

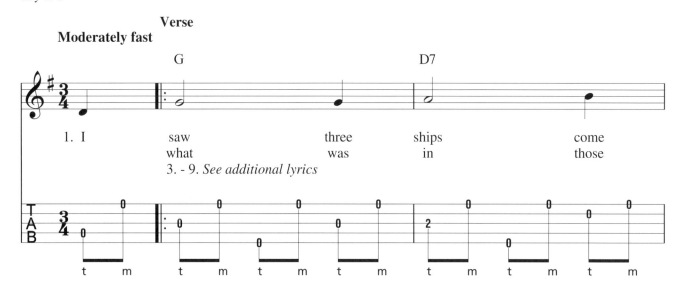

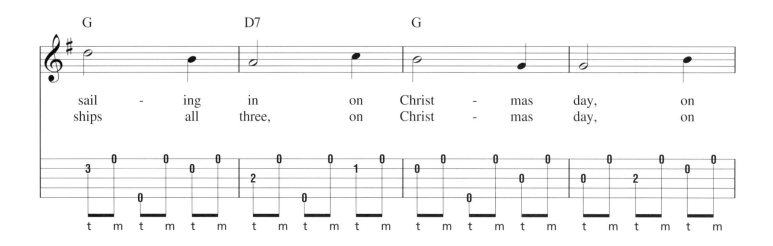

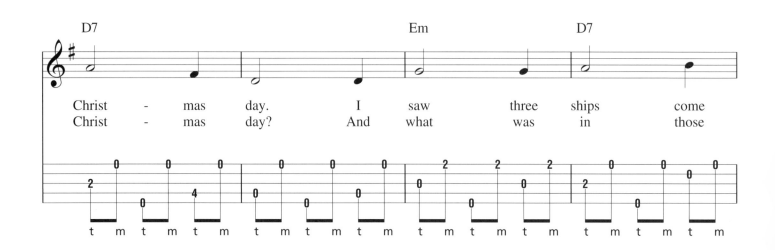

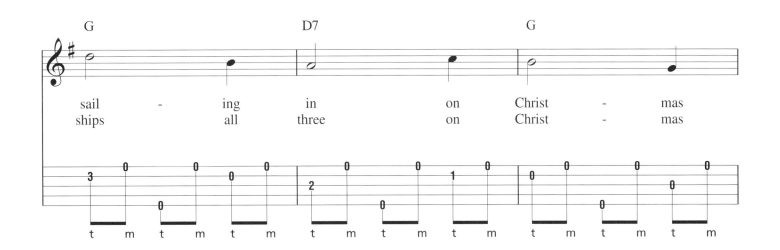

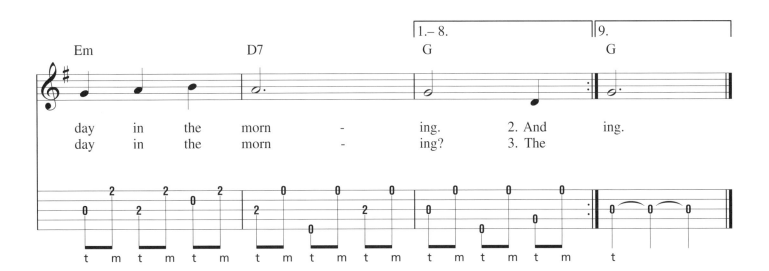

Additional Lyrics

3. The Virgin Mary and Christ were there on Christmas day, on Christmas day.
   The Virgin Mary and Christ were there on Christmas day in the morning.

4. Pray, whither sailed those ships all three on Christmas day, on Christmas day?
   Pray, whither sailed those ships all three on Christmas day in the morning?

5. Oh, they sailed into Bethlehem on Christmas day, on Christmas day.
   Oh, they sailed into Bethlehem on Christmas day in the morning.

6. And all the bells on earth shall ring on Christmas day, on Christmas day.
   And all the bells on earth shall ring on Christmas day in the morning.

7. And all the angels in heaven shall sing on Christmas day, on Christmas day.
   And all the angels in heaven shall sing on Christmas day in the morning.

8. And all the souls on earth shall sing on Christmas day, on Christmas day.
   And all the souls on earth shall sing on Christmas day in the morning.

9. Then let us all rejoice again on Christmas day, on Christmas day.
   Then let us all rejoice again on Christmas day in the morning.

It Came Upon the Midnight Clear

Words by Edmund H. Sears
Traditional English Melody
Adapted by Arthur Sullivan

G tuning:
(5th-1st) G-D-G-B-D

Key of C

Moderately

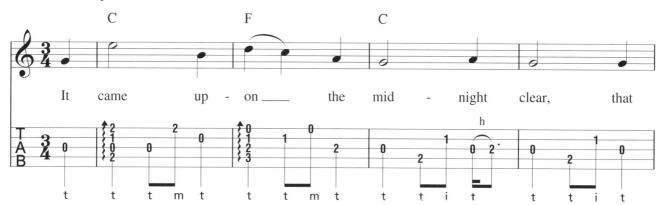

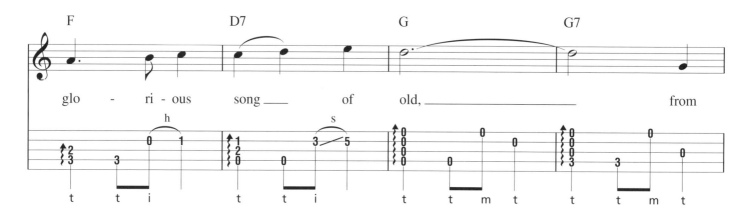

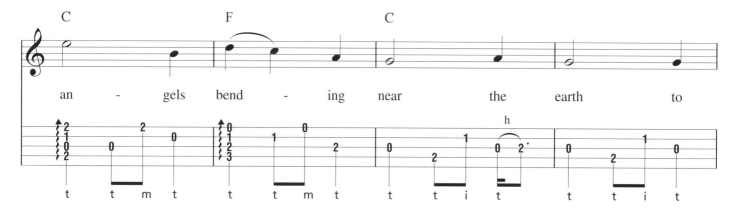

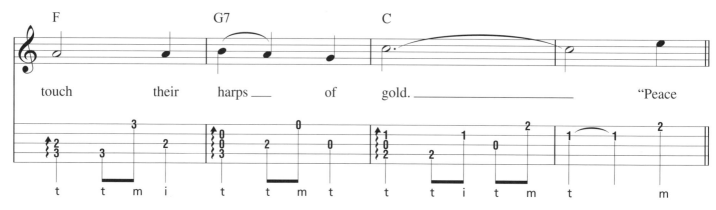

Jingle Bells

Words and Music by J. Pierpont

G tuning:
(5th-1st) G-D-G-B-D

Key of G

Verse

Moderately fast

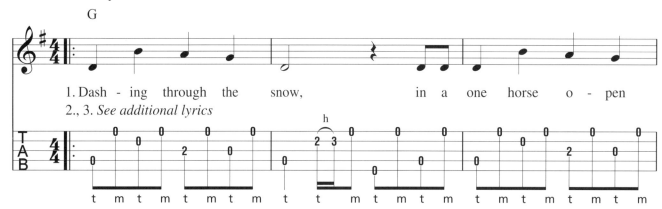

1. Dash - ing through the snow, in a one horse o - pen
2., 3. *See additional lyrics*

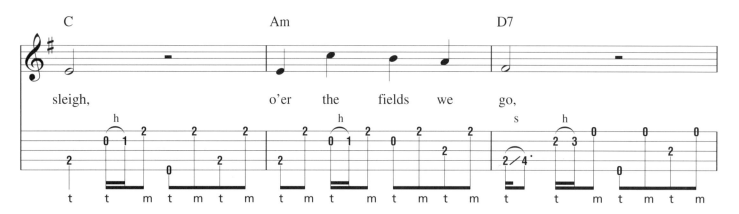

sleigh, o'er the fields we go,

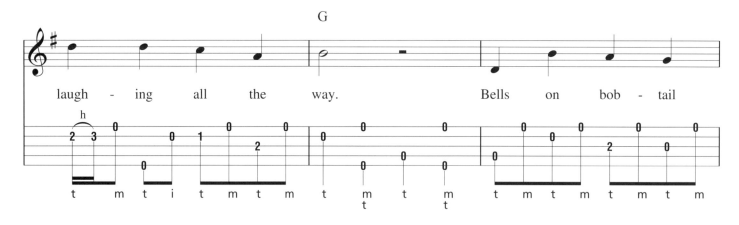

laugh - ing all the way. Bells on bob - tail

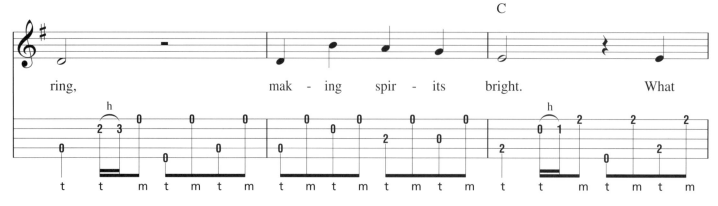

ring, mak - ing spir - its bright. What

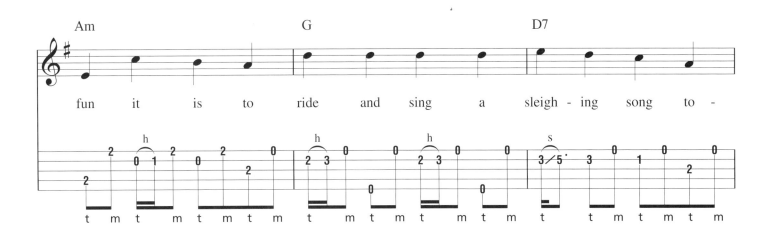

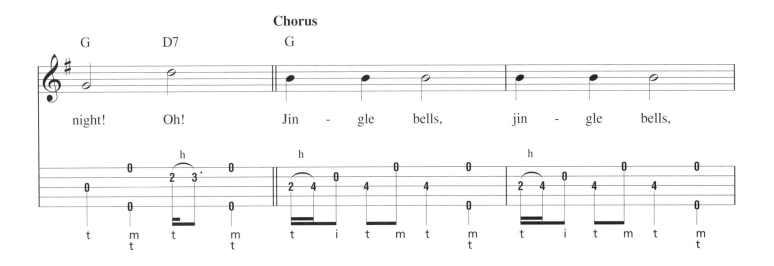

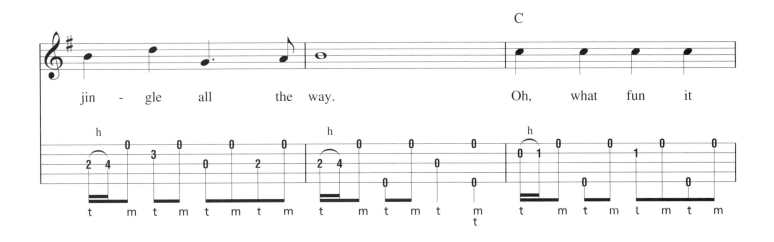

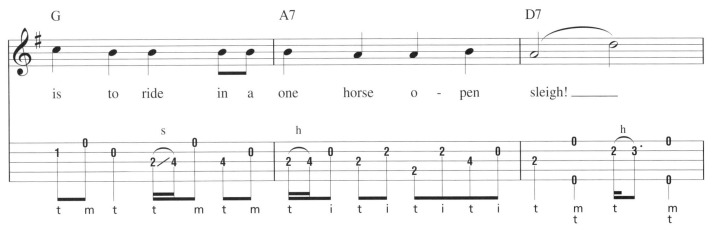

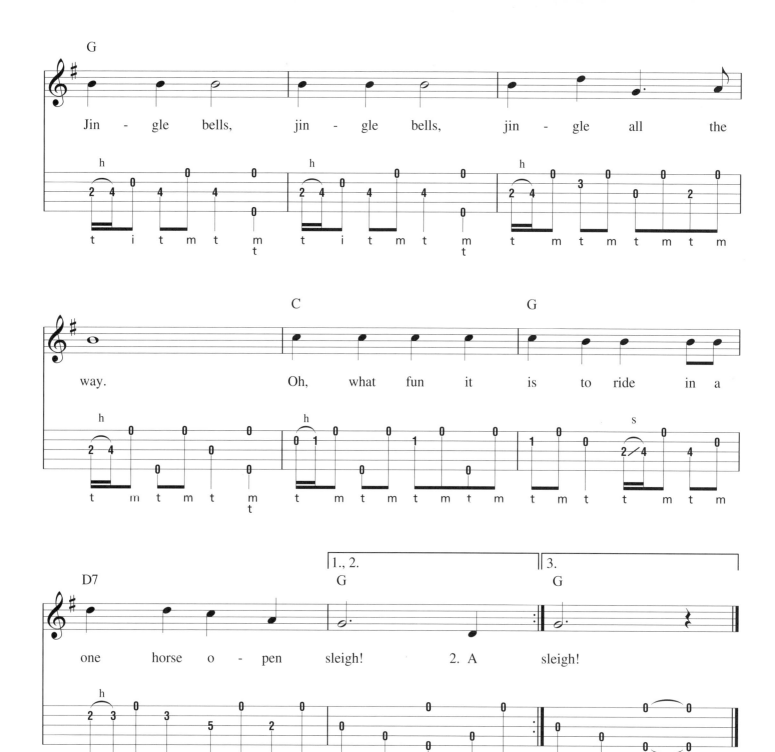

Additional Lyrics

2. A day or two ago, I thought I'd take a ride,
   And soon Miss Fannie Bright was sitting by my side.
   The horse was lean and lank,
   Misfortune seemed his lot.
   He got into a drifted bank and we, we got upshot! Oh!

3. Now the ground is white, go it while you're young.
   Take the girls tonight and sing this sleighing song.
   Just get a bobtail bay,
   Two-forty for his speed.
   Then hitch him to an open sleigh and crack, you'll take the lead! Oh!

What Child Is This?

Words by William C. Dix
16th Century English Melody

G minor tuning:
(5th-1st) G-D-G-B♭-D
Key of Gm

Verse
Moderately slow

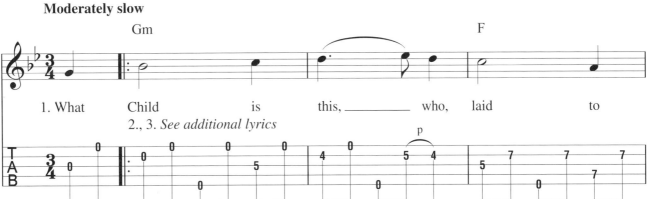

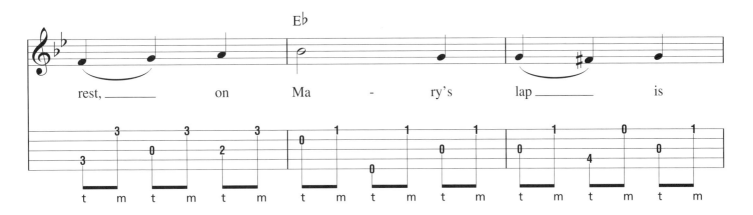

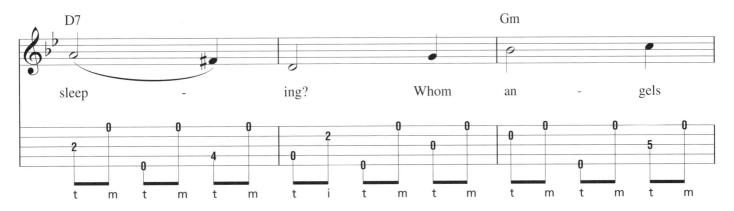

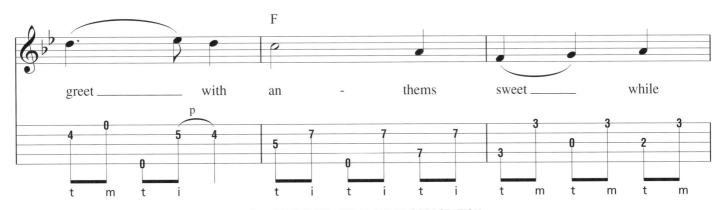

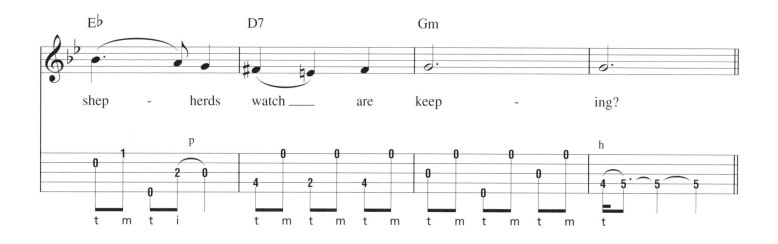

Chorus

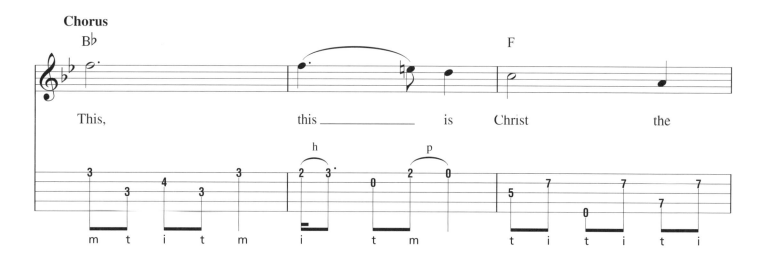

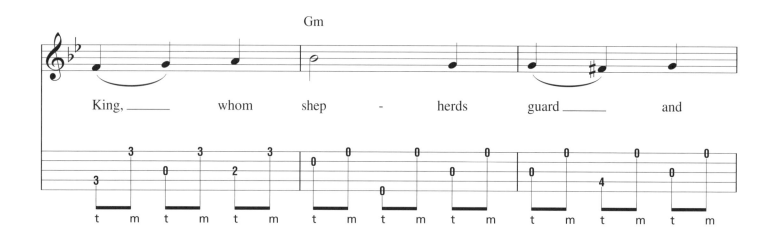

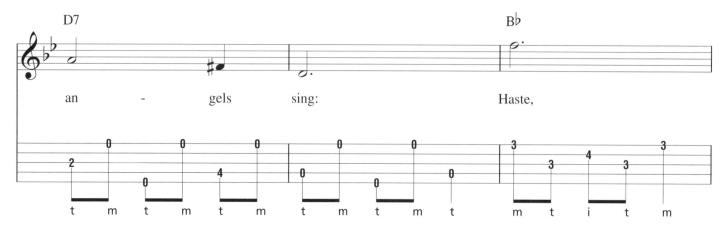

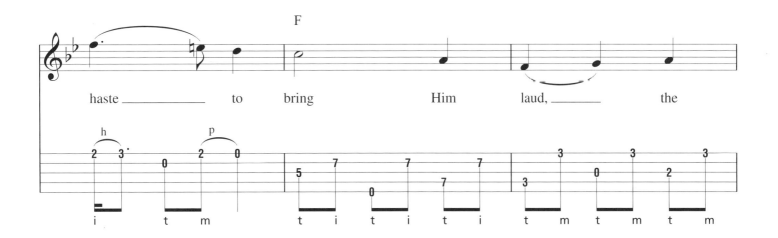

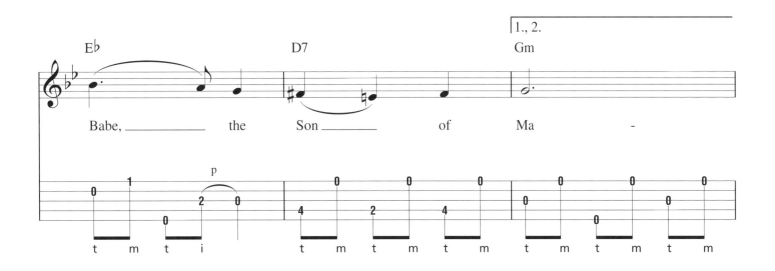

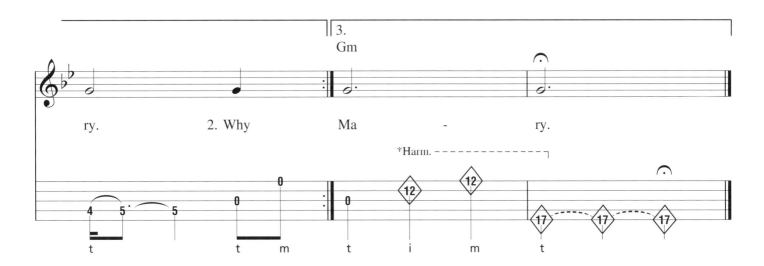

Additional Lyrics

2. Why lies He in such mean estate
   Where ox and ass are feeding?
   Good Christian, fear, for sinners here
   The silent word is pleading.

3. So bring Him incense, gold and myrrh.
   Come, peasant King, to own Him.
   The King of Kings salvation brings,
   Let loving hearts enthrone Him.

*Harmonics are produced by picking the note while the fret-hand lightly touches the strings over the fret indicated.

Jolly Old St. Nicholas

Traditional 19th Century American Carol

G tuning:
(5th-1st) G-D-G-B-D
Key of G

Verse

Moderately fast

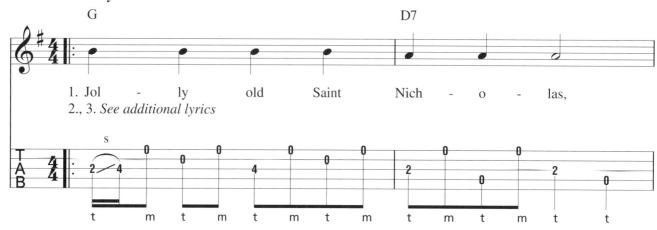

1. Jol - ly old Saint Nich - o - las,
2., 3. *See additional lyrics*

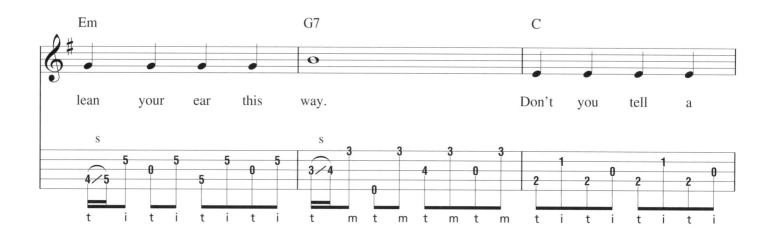

lean your ear this way. Don't you tell a

sin - gle soul what I'm going to say.

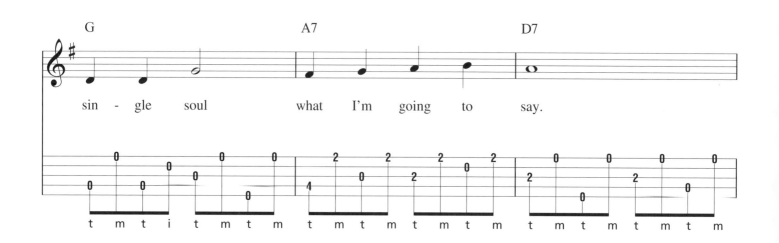

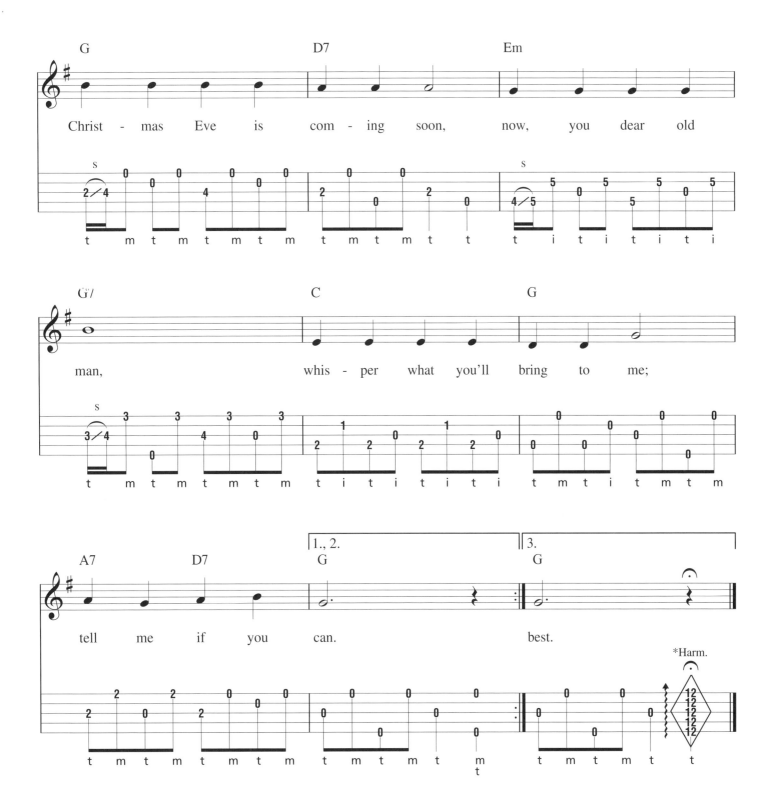

Additional Lyrics

2.   When the clock is striking twelve, when I'm fast asleep,
Down the chimney broad and black, with your pack you'll creep.
All the stockings you will find hanging in a row.
Mine will be the shortest one, you'll be sure to know.

3.   Johnny wants a pair of skates; Suzy wants a sled.
Nellie wants a picture book, yellow, blue and red.
Now I think I'll leave to you what to give the rest.
Choose for me, dear Santa Claus, you will know the best.

*Harmonics are produced by picking the notes while the fret-hand lightly touches the strings over the fret indicated.

Joy to the World

Words by Isaac Watts
Music by George Frideric Handel
Arranged by Lowell Mason

G tuning:
(5th-1st) G-D-G-B-D

Key of G

Verse

Moderately fast

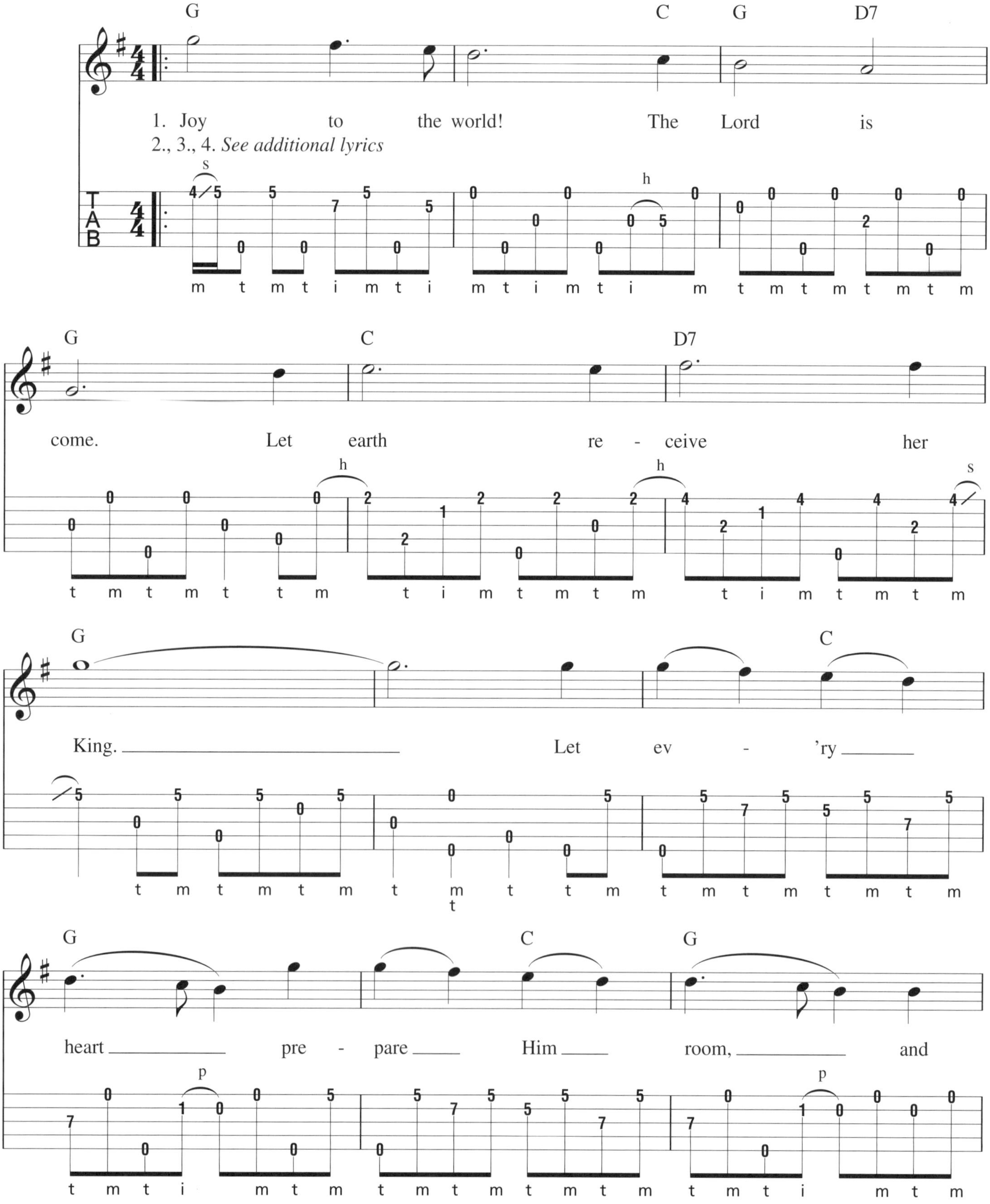

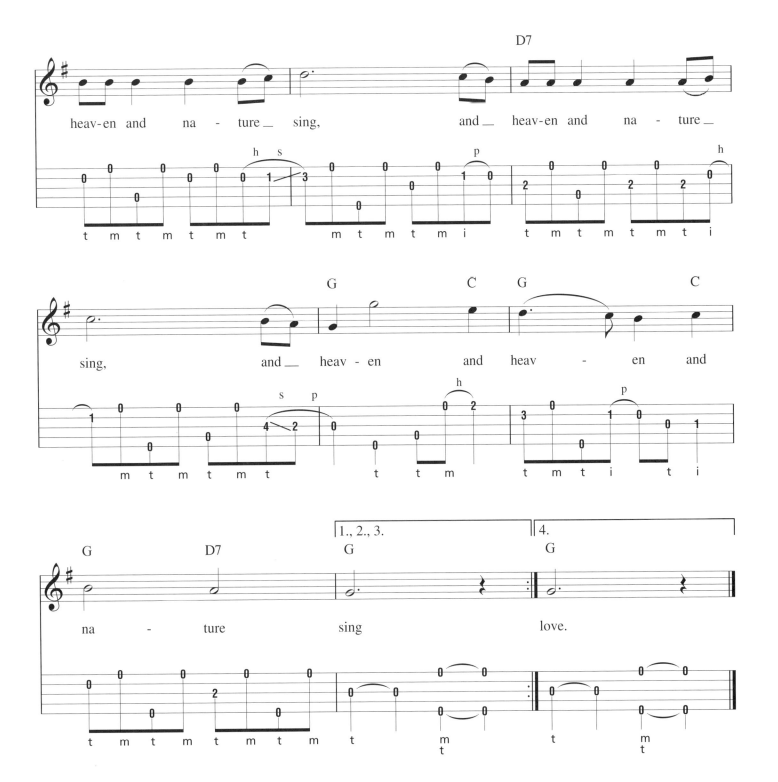

Additional Lyrics

2. Joy to the world! The Savior reigns.
   Let men their songs employ;
   While fields and floods, rocks, hills and plains
   Repeat the sounding joy,
   Repeat the sounding joy,
   Repeat, repcat the sounding joy.

3. No more let sin and sorrow grow,
   Nor thorns infest the ground.
   He comes to make His blessings flow
   Far as the curse is found,
   Far as the curse is found,
   Far as, far as the curse is found.

4. He rules the world with truth and grace,
   And makes the nations prove
   The glories of His righteousness,
   And wonders of His love,
   And wonders of His love,
   And wonders, wonders of His love.

O Christmas Tree

Traditional German Carol

G tuning:
(5th-1st) G-D-G-B-D

Key of C

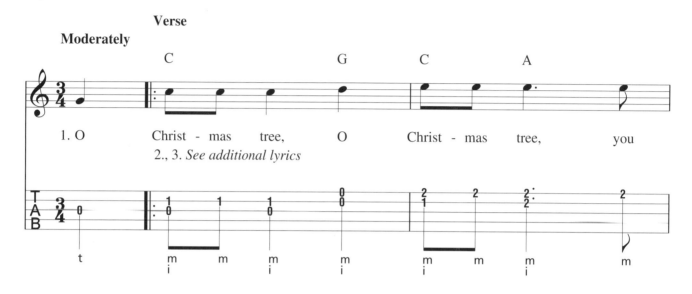

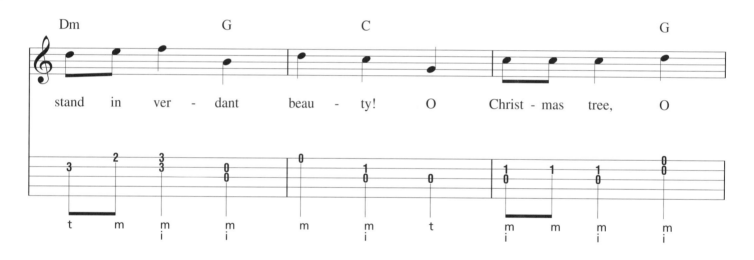

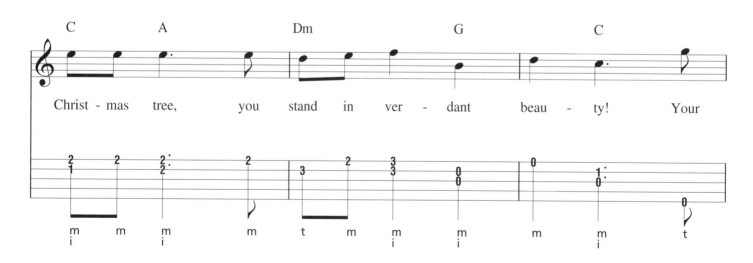

Additional Lyrics

2. O Christmas tree! O Christmas tree,
   Much pleasure doth thou bring me!
   O Christmas tree! O Christmas tree,
   Much pleasure doth thou bring me!
   For every year the Christmas tree
   Brings to us all both joy and glee.
   O Christmas tree! O Christmas tree,
   Much pleasure doth thou bring me!

3. O Christmas tree! O Christmas tree,
   Thy candles shine out brightly!
   O Christmas tree! O Christmas tree,
   Thy candles shine out brightly!
   Each bough doth hold its tiny light
   That makes each toy to sparkle bright.
   O Christmas tree! O Christmas tree,
   Thy candles shine out brightly!

O Come, All Ye Faithful
(Adeste Fideles)

Words and Music by John Francis Wade
Latin Words translated by Frederick Oakeley

G tuning:
(5th-1st) G-D-G-B-D

Key of G

Verse

Moderately

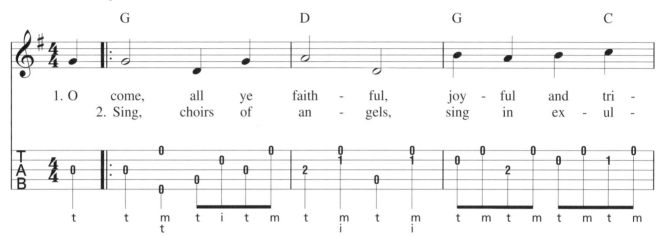

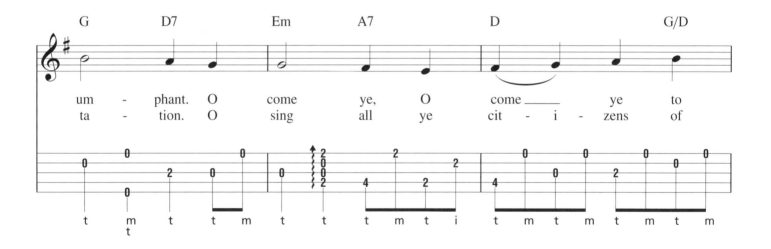

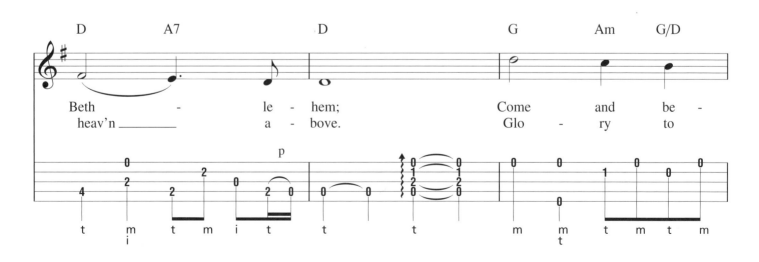

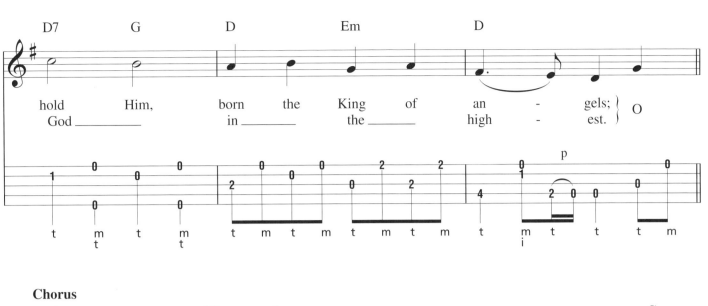

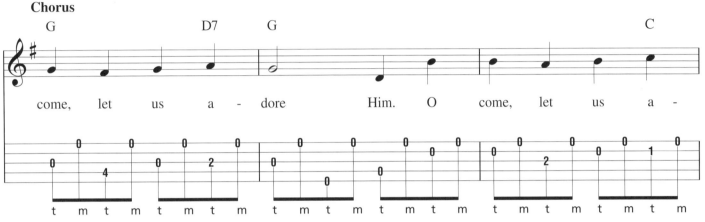

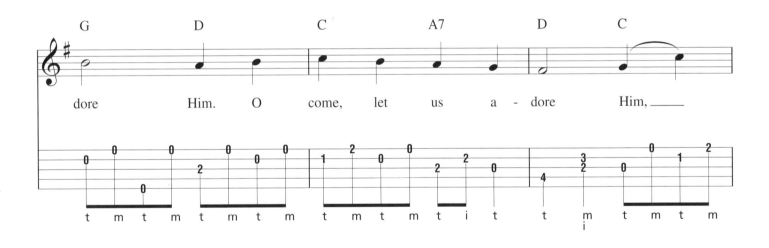

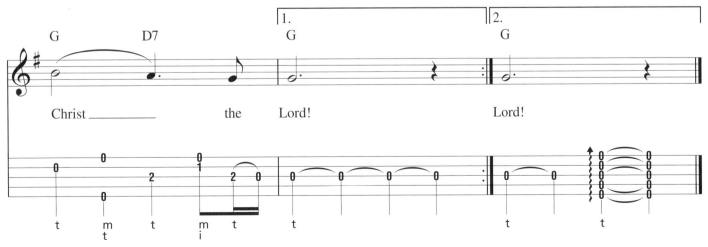

O Come, O Come, Emmanuel

Traditional Latin Text
V. 1,2 translated by John M. Neale
V. 3,4 translated by Henry S. Coffin
15th Century French Melody
Adapted by Thomas Helmore

G tuning:
(5th-1st) G-D-G-B-D

Key of Em

Verse

Moderately

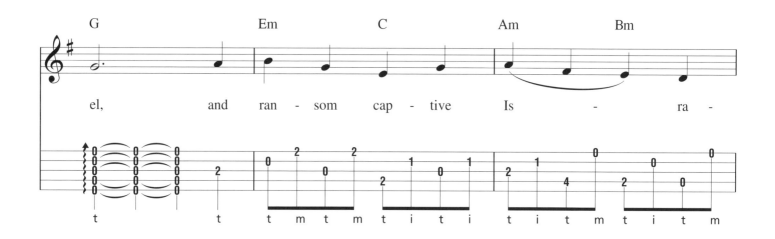

1. O come, O come, Imman - u -
2., 3. *See additional lyrics*

el, and ran - som cap - tive Is - ra -

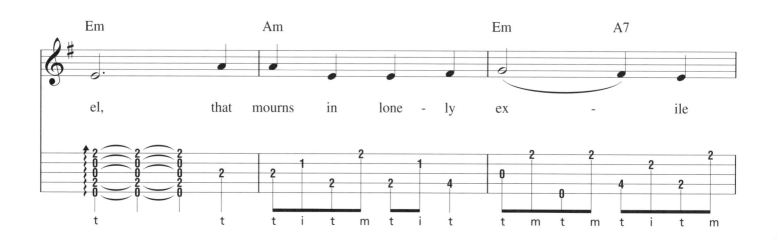

el, that mourns in lone - ly ex - ile

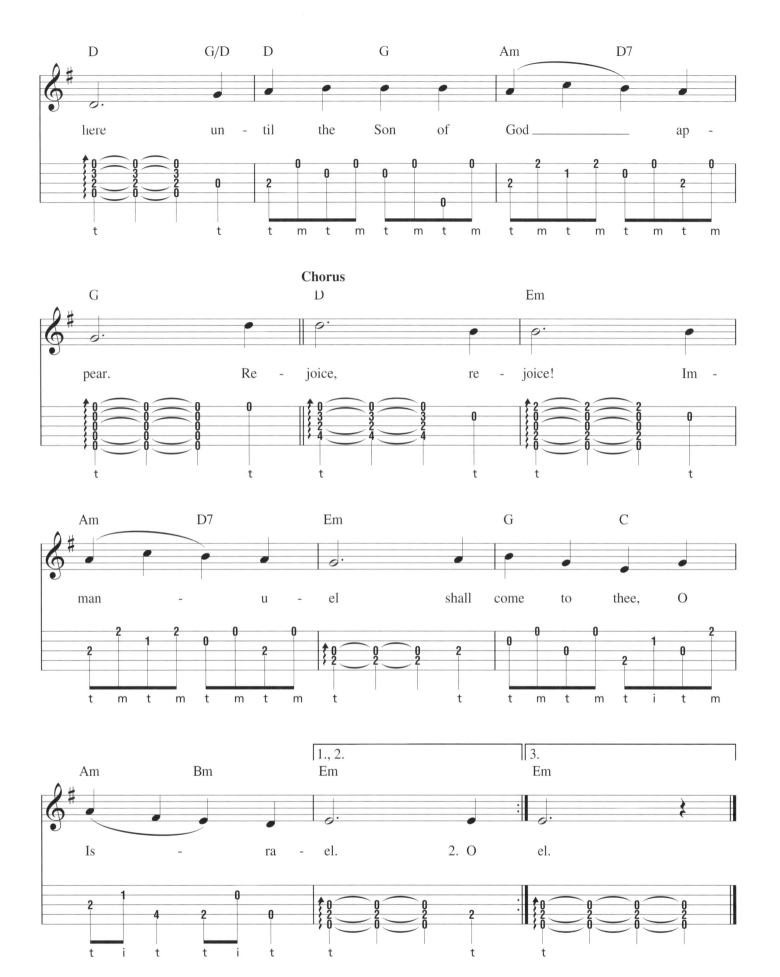

Additional Lyrics

2. O come, Thou Wisdom from on high,
   And order all things far and nigh;
   To us, the path of knowledge show
   And cause us in her ways to go.

3. O come, Desire of Nations, bind
   All people in one heart and mind;
   Bid envy, strife, and quarrel's cease;
   Fill the whole world with heaven's peace.

O Holy Night

French Words by Placide Cappeau
English Words by John S. Dwight
Music by Adolphe Adam

G tuning:
(5th-1st) G-D-G-B-D

Key of G

Intro
Moderately

Verse

1. O Ho - ly night _____ the stars are bright - ly shin -
2. Tru - ly He taught us to love _____ one an - oth -

ing, it is the night of the dear Sav - ior's birth. _____
er. His law is love, and His gos - pel is peace. _____

_____ Long lay the world _____ in sin and er - ror
_____ Chains shall He break, for the slave _____ is our

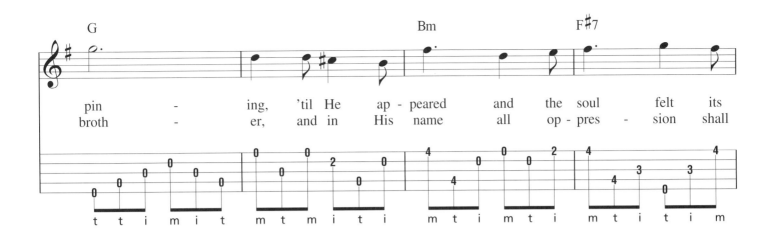

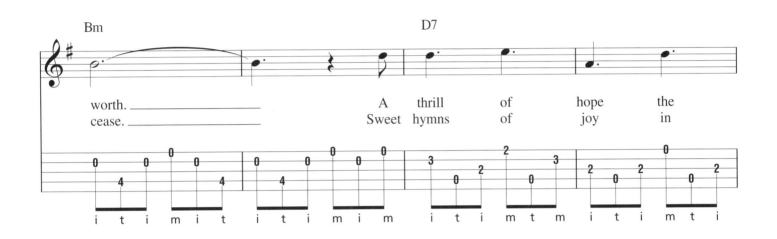

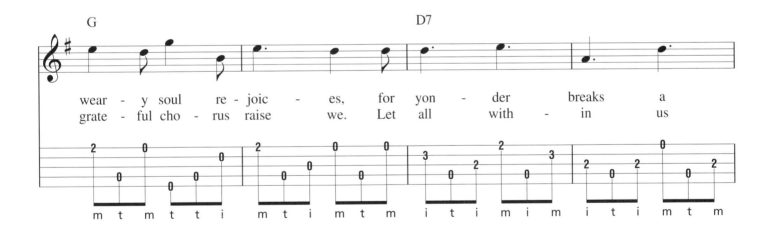

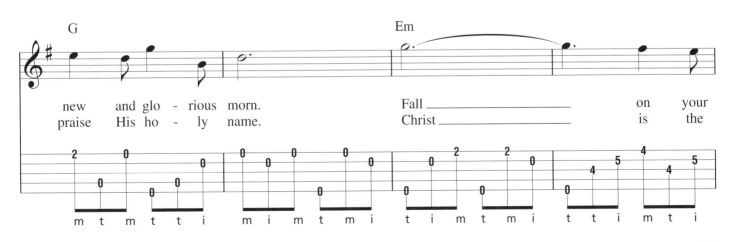

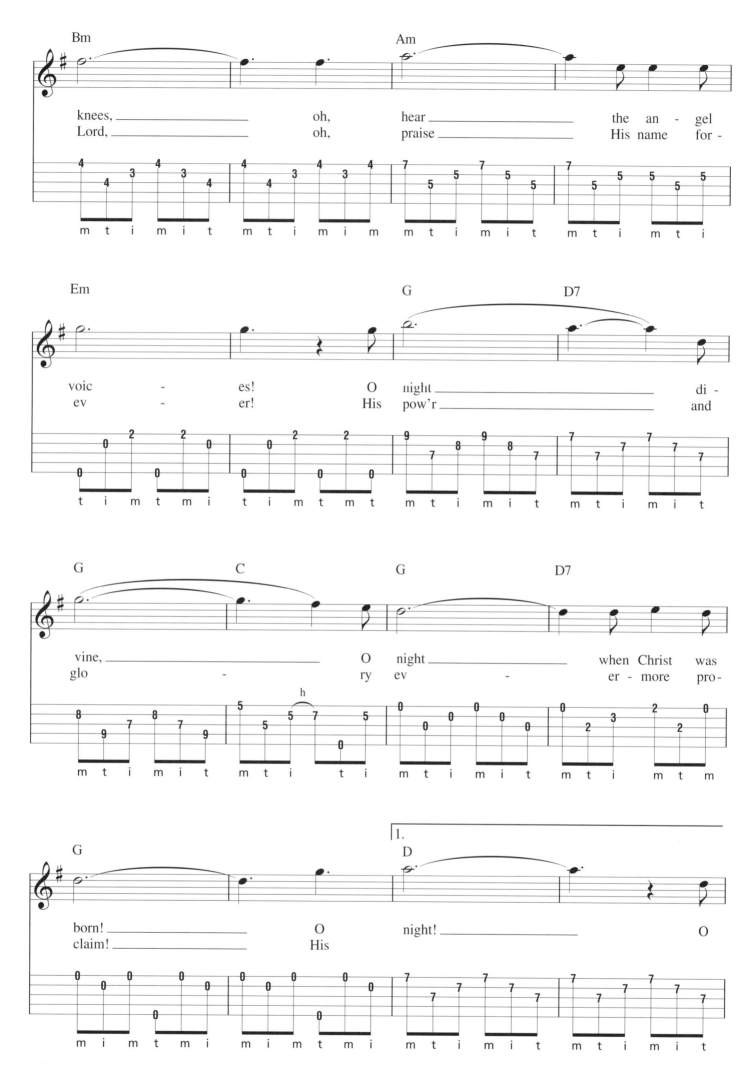

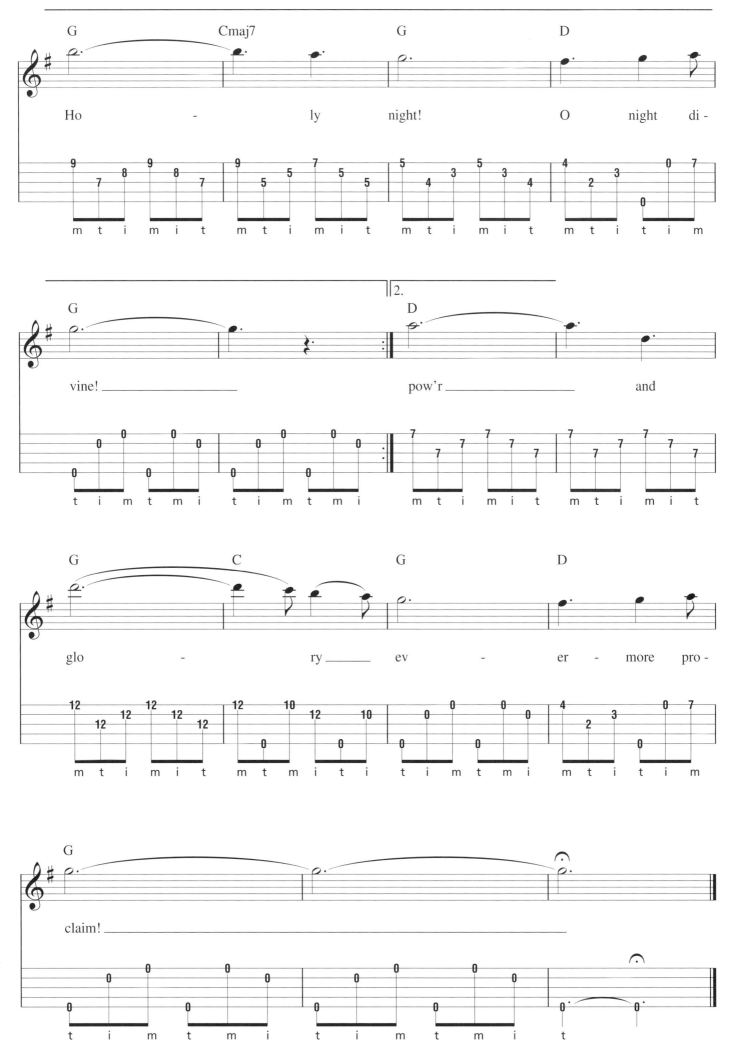

O Little Town of Bethlehem

Words by Phillips Brooks
Music by Lewis H. Redner

G tuning:
(5th-1st) G-D-G-B-D

Key of G

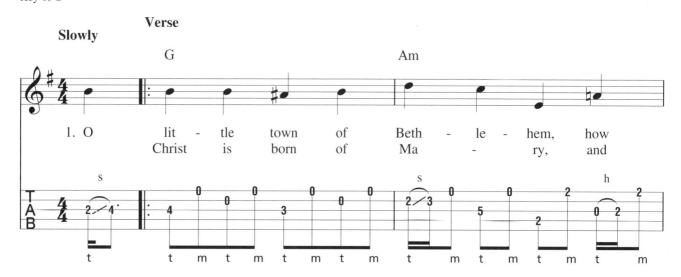

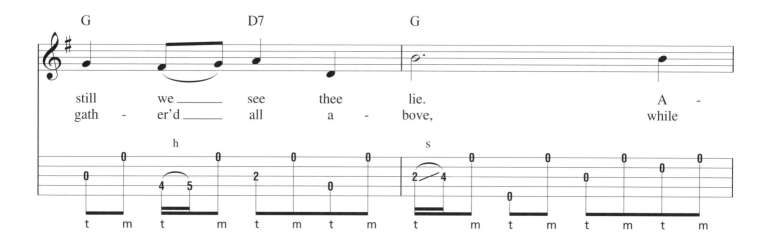

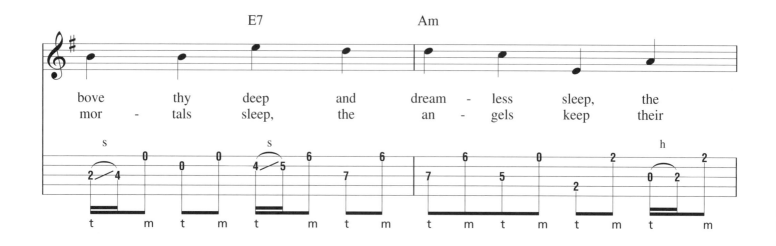

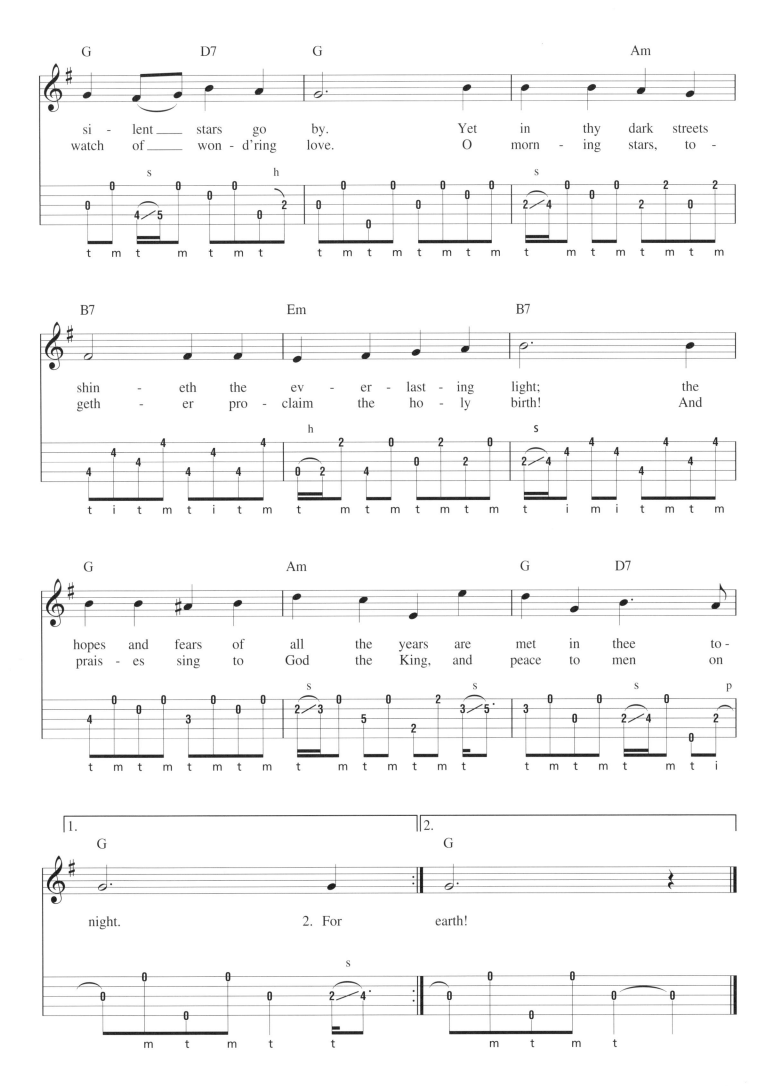

Silent Night

Words by Joseph Mohr
Translated by John F. Young
Music by Franz X. Gruber

G tuning:
(5th-1st) G-D-G-B-D

Key of D

Verse

Moderately slow

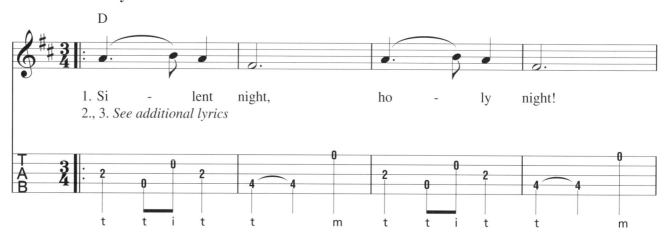

1. Si - lent night, ho - ly night!
2., 3. *See additional lyrics*

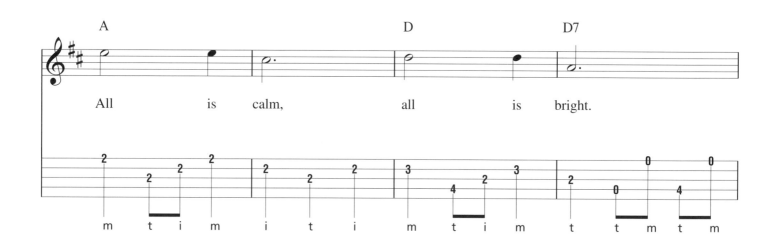

All is calm, all is bright.

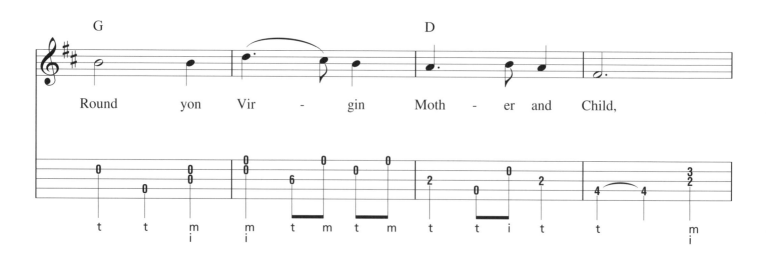

Round yon Vir - gin Moth - er and Child,

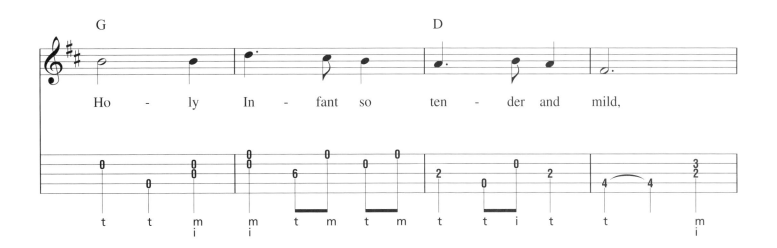

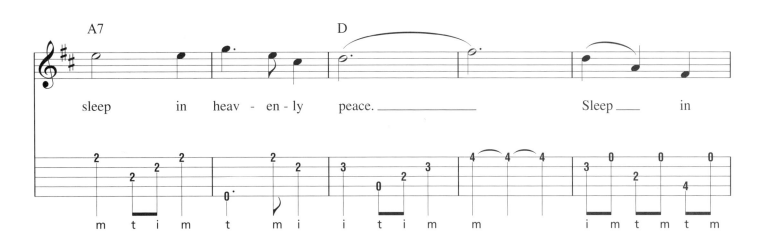

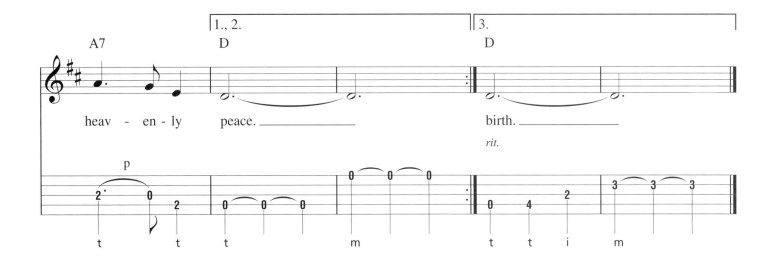

Additional Lyrics

2. Silent night, holy night!
Shepherds quake at the sight.
Glories stream from heaven afar.
Heavenly hosts sing Allelulia.
Christ the Savior is born!
Christ the Savior is born!

3. Silent night, holy night!
Son of God, love's pure light.
Radiant beams from Thy holy face
With the dawn of redeeming grace,
Jesus Lord at Thy birth.
Jesus Lord at Thy birth.

Up on the Housetop

Words and Music by B.R. Handy

Chorus

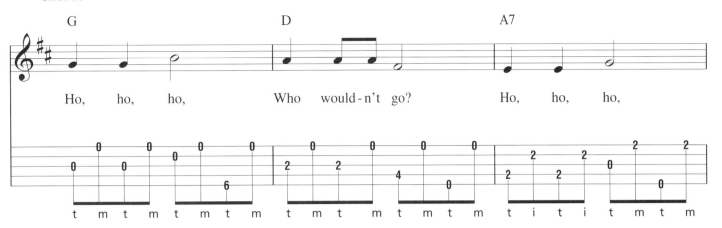

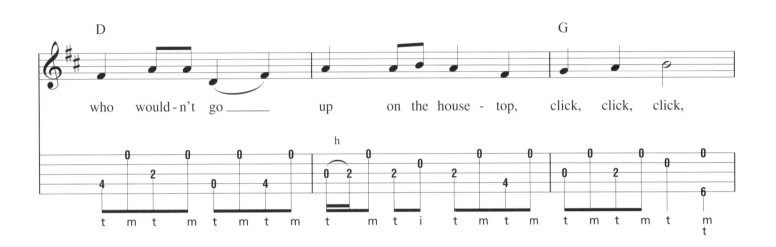

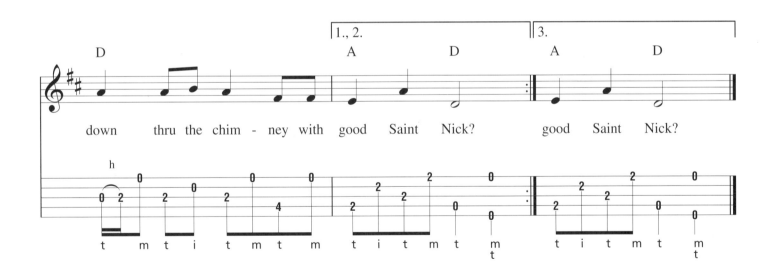

Additional Lyrics

2. First comes the stocking of little Nell,
   Oh, dear Santa, fill it well.
   Give her a dollie that laughs and cries,
   One that will open and shut her eyes.

3. Next comes the stocking of little Will,
   Oh, just see what a glorious fill!
   Here is a hammer and lots of tacks,
   Also a ball and a whip that cracks.

We Three Kings of Orient Are

Words and Music by John H. Hopkins, Jr.

Chorus

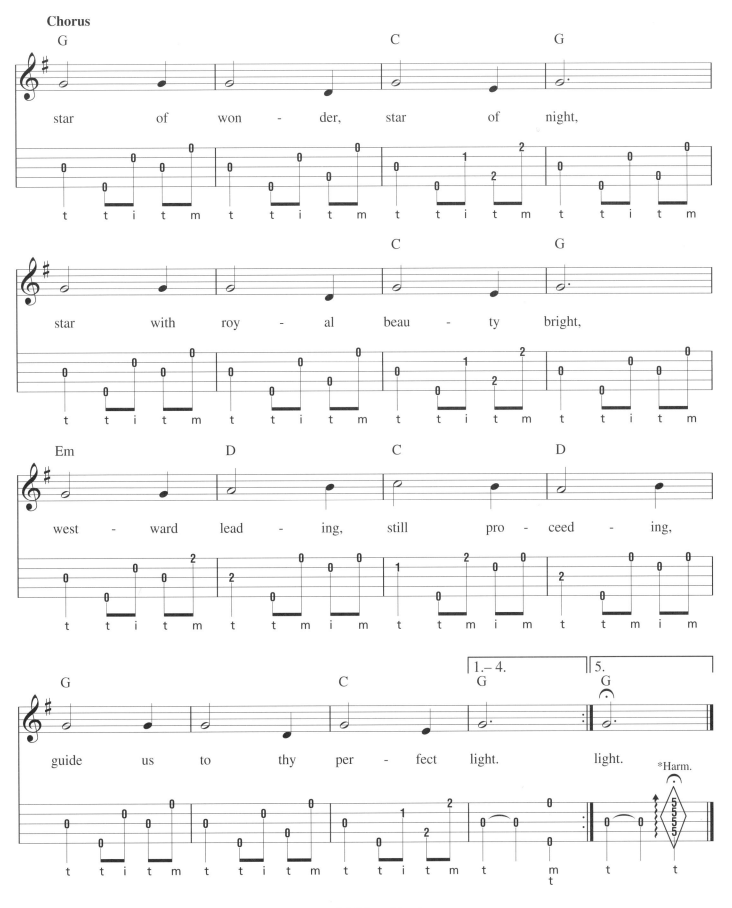

Additional Lyrics

3. Frankincense to offer have I;
   Incense owns a Deity nigh;
   Prayer and praising, all men raising,
   Worship Him, God most high.

4. Myrrh us mine: it's bitter perfume
   Breathes a life of gathering gloom:
   Sorrowing, sighing, bleeding, dying:
   Sealed in the stone-cold tomb.

5. Glorious now, behold Him arise,
   King and God, and Sacrifice!
   Heav'n sings alleluia,
   Alleluia the earth replies:

*Harmonics are produced by picking the notes while the fret-hand lightly touches the strings over the fret indicated.

We Wish You a Merry Christmas

Traditional English Folksong

G tuning:
(5th-1st) G-D-G-B-D

Key of G

Moderately fast

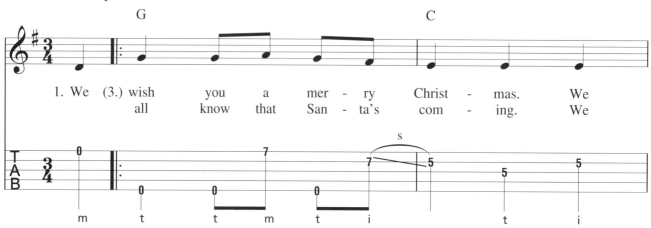

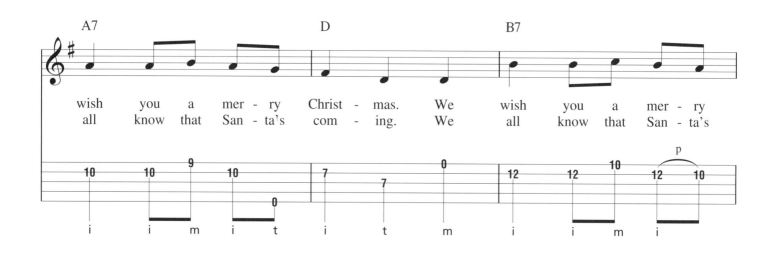

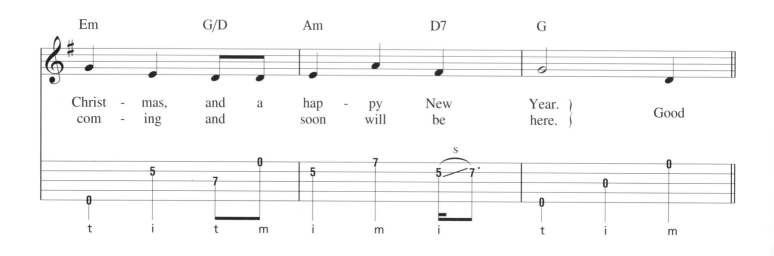

Banjo Notation Legend

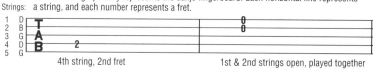

TABLATURE graphically represents the banjo fingerboard. Each horizontal line represents a string, and each number represents a fret.

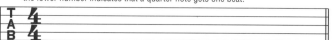

4th string, 2nd fret   1st & 2nd strings open, played together

TIME SIGNATURE:
The upper number indicates the number of beats per measure, the lower number indicates that a quarter note gets one beat.

CUT TIME:
Each note's time value should be cut in half. As a result, the music will be played twice as fast as it is written.

QUARTER NOTE:
time value = 1 beat

EIGHTH NOTES:
time value = 1/2 beat each

single   in series

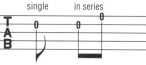

SIXTEENTH NOTES:
time value = 1/4 beat each

single   in series

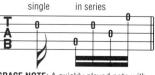

DOTTED QUARTER NOTE:
time value = 1 1/2 beat

TIE: Pick the 1st note only, then let it sustain for the combined time value.

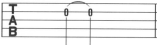

TRIPLET: Three notes played in the same time normally occupied by two notes of the same time value.

GRACE NOTE: A quickly played note with no time value of its own. The grace note and the note following it only occupy the time value of the second note.

RITARD: A gradual slowing of the tempo or speed of the song.

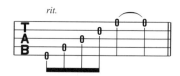

QUARTER REST:
time value = 1 beat of silence

EIGHTH REST:
time value = 1/2 beat of silence

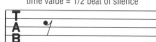

HALF REST:
time value = 2 beats of silence

WHOLE REST:
time value = 4 beats of silence

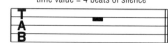

ENDINGS: When a repeated section has a first and second ending, play the first ending only the first time and play the second ending only the second time.

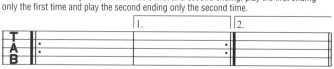

REPEAT SIGNS: Play the music between the repeat signs two times.

D.S. AL CODA:
Play through the music until you complete the measure labeled *"D.S. al Coda,"* then go back to the sign (𝄋).
Then play until you complete the measure labeled *"To Coda ⊕,"* then skip to the section labeled "⊕ *Coda.*"

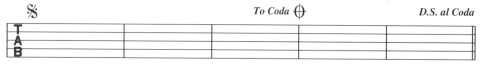

HAMMER-ON: Strike the first (lower) note with one finger, then sound the higher note (on the same string) with another finger by fretting it without picking.

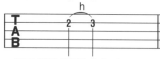

PULL-OFF: Place both fingers on the notes to be sounded. Strike the first note and without picking, pull the finger off to sound the second (lower) note.

SLIDE UP: Strike the first note and then slide the same fret-hand finger up to the second note. The second note is not struck.

SLIDE DOWN: Strike the first note and then slide the same fret-hand finger down to the second note. The second note is not struck.

HALF-STEP CHOKE: Strike the note and bend the string up 1/2 step.

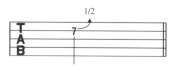

WHOLE-STEP CHOKE: Strike the note and bend the string up one step.

NATURAL HARMONIC: Strike the note while the fret-hand lightly touches the string directly over the fret indicated.

BRUSH: Play the notes of the chord indicated by quickly rolling them from bottom to top.

Scruggs/Keith Tuners:

HALF-TWIST UP: Strike the note, twist tuner up 1/2 step, and continue playing.

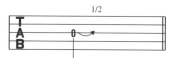

HALF-TWIST DOWN: Strike the note, twist tuner down 1/2 step, and continue playing.

WHOLE-TWIST UP: Strike the note, twist tuner up one step, and continue playing.

Right Hand Fingerings

t = thumb   i = index finger   m = middle finger